HOW TO HAVE
A
WELL-MANNERED DOG

D1578595

Also available from Elliot Right Way Books

Choose & Bring Up Your Puppy
The Right Way To Keep Cats
The Right Way To Keep Rabbits
The Right Way To Keep Hamsters
The Right Way To Keep Pet Fish

All uniform with this book

HOW TO HAVE A WELL-MANNERED DOG

Kay White & J M Evans MRCVS

RIGHT WAY

Copyright notice

© Elliot Right Way Books MCMLXXXI
First published in the *Right Way* series © MCMXCVI

All rights reserved. No part of this book may be reproduced, stored in a retrieval system, or transmitted, in any form or by any means, electronic, photocopying, mechanical, recording or otherwise, without the prior permission of the copyright owner.

Conditions of sale
This book shall only be sold, lent, or hired, for profit, trade, or otherwise, in its original binding, except where special permission has been granted by the Publishers.

Whilst care is taken in selecting Authors who are authoritative in their subjects, it is emphasised that their books can reflect their knowledge only up to the time of writing. Information can be superseded and printers' errors can creep in. This book is sold, therefore, on the condition that neither Publisher nor Author can be held legally responsible for the consequences of any error or omission there may be.

Typeset in 11/12pt Times by Letterpart Ltd., Reigate, Surrey.

Printed and bound in Great Britain by Cox & Wyman Ltd., Reading, Berkshire.

The *Right Way* series and the *Paperfronts* series are both published by Elliot Right Way Books, Brighton Road, Lower Kingswood, Tadworth, Surrey, KT20 6TD, U.K.

CONTENTS

DEDICATION

To Anna the Doberman, and Pixie, Tigger, Pooka,
Berry and Holly the Boxers and
ALL GOOD DOGS!

ACKNOWLEDGMENTS

Illustrations by Harold White

Cover photograph courtesy of Ardea London Ltd,
35 Brodrick Road, Wandsworth Common,
London SW17 7DX

INTRODUCTION

For thousands of years we have been content to have dogs as our companions, to admire them, to love them, and to rely upon them to protect us and to help us in our work and our sporting pursuits.

It is only relatively recently that we have begun to study the way a dog's mind works, the way he learns and the way a dog interprets our own actions. In our over-crowded and busy world it is getting more and more difficult to keep pets. People can and do complain about even well intentioned dogs which bounce up to them in parks, bark at them from behind your own fence, or appear to threaten legitimate callers to your home. Such complaints can easily lead to court proceedings, so it is in your own interests to make sure that your dog causes no annoyance to anyone.

It is fortunate that we now have the benefit of studies, originally made in the United States and now going on in many countries, including Britain, into the natural behaviour patterns of dogs and their responses to human beings. Years of experience with our own dogs have made us aware that it is possible to bring up puppies to be fun-loving, but well-behaved members of a family group without the need for harsh, regimented training. We bring up puppies as we do children, to be aware of the limits of permissible behaviour, and to be aware when they are pleasing us and, equally, when they are on the verge of doing wrong.

We speak not of training puppies but of educating and managing them. We believe that if you follow the advice in this book your new puppy will have much less chance of acquiring bad habits which annoy you and other people. And even if your own dog has already acquired annoying, frustrating and even dangerous habits we believe that if you follow our methods you can turn such an animal into an enjoyable pet; a dog which will feel secure and contented about its position in the family pack. Dogs value, and positively need, their owner's approval and we hope that once we have put you and your dog on the same wavelength you will be able to communicate easily and so be happy together.

This book is written by two authors, and between us we have a wide knowledge of the world of dogs. One, JM Evans, is a veterinary surgeon. The other, Kay White, for many years owned a boarding and breeding kennel and has always lived in a multi-dog household, latterly with a crowd of Boxers.

Dog management our way does not take a lot of time, but on the other hand, it is not a magic formula which works immediately. You do not need to take your dog to training classes or learn the military drill which earns high marks in obedience competitions for those dogs and their owners who have aptitude and ambition in this sphere.

The secret of dog management our way is all a matter of approaching your puppy in the right way and programming your pet to fit in with your way of life. Our management programme starts early, on the first day you take a puppy into your home, or even, although this is harder work for both owner and dog, you can begin with a dog which already has behaviour problems. This book will help you to understand your dog and will teach you to act in such a way that your dog can understand you. From there, the whole world of dog ability is open to you, or you may just settle for happy companionship with a well-behaved but lively and joyous dog which is the envy of all your friends.

If you have a dog which has already learnt that being a nuisance brings its own rewards, we will show you that clever remedial work will bring you a dog you can really enjoy . . . you *can* teach an old dog, or at least a middle-aged dog, new tricks. Dogs are exceedingly adaptable, thousands of years of living close to man has honed that skill, but dogs need to know where they fit into a household and what is required of them. They need a consistency of management to give them a feeling of security in the environment in which they live. So when you start your programme of dog management you must beware of allowing a privilege 'just this once.'

Your Promise To The Dog

Your commitment in taking on a dog should include:

* Feeding and grooming properly and regularly.
* Consulting a veterinary surgeon when you see signs of illness.
* Taking out veterinary fee insurance cover to help with the major bills if your dog becomes seriously ill or has an accident.
* Making sure the dog has protective vaccinations.
* Providing a collar and name tag with your own current address which must always be worn when the dog is outside your own house and garden.
* Providing sufficient exercise and constructive playtime.
* Considering having your male dog neutered or your bitch spayed early in life so that there is no risk of unwanted litters.
* Making arrangements to have your dog properly looked after when you cannot do so yourself.
* And realising that you have a commitment to make the dog a part of your family until the end of its days.

It is a sad aspect of modern society that people often seek to shed the commitment they have made to an animal on the thinnest of excuses, but they say they feel sure that someone else will be able to 'give it a good home' despite the fact that the dog has no house-manners at all. Many of the pathetic dogs in rescue homes are *people failures*, the victims of people who did not keep their promises, spoken or unspoken, to care for the dog for ever, including teaching it to be an acceptable animal in today's world.

Owning a dog is one of the great pleasures of life, mainly because the dog takes up the slack where human companionship, collaboration and devotion fall short. It is a rare thing indeed for a dog to fail to keep its unspoken promise of devotion to its owner and its owner's immediate family.

Dogs give unconditional trust and affection. They are uncritical of our failings and they give the same rapturous welcome always without reproach regardless of our shortcomings.

Dogs take years off your age by providing a compelling reason to take outdoor exercise, and also by allowing us to play in a child-like way without looking silly . . . a dog makes the ideal excuse.

A dog makes friends for you. When out with your dog you may speak to people and receive their cordiality in return in a way that would be impossible with non-dog owners.

A dog is a safety-valve in many relationships, and sometimes the only bridge across which people can communicate.

For an only or lonely child, the warm affectionate dog can be anything the imagination allows, from a magic animal with supernatural powers, to a confidant, a consoler, an agile and enthusiastic playmate, a loyal companion to share the burden of naughtiness, a friend that licks and never tells, or a possession to boast about, a status symbol for a child or older person where enhancement of their own self-image is needed.

We need dogs, and dogs need people, for our mutual benefit.

Section I

DOGS, THEIR NATURE & CHARACTERISTICS

1

MAN & DOG

It was probably not long after the first man/dog friendships were formed, long before recorded history, that man realised that dog had a range of talents which could be put to good use. Very soon, fast-running dogs were being bred together to provide offspring which would excel at chasing gazelle and deer. Dogs with long noses and wide nostrils proved good at following scent and they helped track down game. Big dogs with heavy shoulders could pull carts, little dogs with flexible bodies could flush rodents out of holes, dogs that were possessive about their kill could be taught to guard their master's property too. Down the centuries, dogs were specially selected and bred together for their working ability, and those that did not make the grade became pets for children.

The body shape and the fur covering of the dog has been manipulated as no other animal's has been. Sometimes new breeds of dog were introduced to be specially suitable for a purpose, sometimes just to fill the eye with an object of beauty, sometimes, as in the case of the regional terriers such as West Highland Whites, Yorkshire Terriers and Border Terriers, just for the sake of having something different from the next town, or the next district.

The cult of specialist designed dogs reached its peak at the end of the nineteenth century when breeds which we know so well today, like the Boxer, the Doberman, the Yorkshire Terrier and the Boston Terrier were deliberately evolved from other canine 'ingredients'. The dog designers wanted character traits as well as body shape and they planned the ancestry to provide both aspects in the dog they created. We may no longer want the working ability which was built into the dog, but we have to realise that we cannot avoid taking the inborn character as a package deal with the body shape we admire.

When choosing a dog it is possible to select away from the traits we require least. If we do not have super safe acres of running space, we may decide that the elegant Saluki and the other high speed movers are not for us. If there are aggressive male dogs living next door, it would be unwise to choose a male Boxer or other dominant breed which might be inclined to do battle through the fence.

The same in-built ability and character trends are present in the cross bred mongrel but there you have more of the lucky-dip situation in that you may not know the ingredients or how they will combine. Some crosses seem to produce conflict within the dog itself, for instance the genial gun-dog mated to a guard-dog may never settle into an easy role in life.

The twentieth century has proved good to dogs in some ways, providing better nutrition in commercially produced diets, enormous advances in veterinary knowledge and skills, and protective vaccination which prevents early death from infectious disease. But conversely, busy roads mean that dogs cannot be allowed their freedom to wander loose as once they did. A more hygiene-conscious population has brought about by-laws which forbid dogs on beaches during the summer, and dogs are not allowed now in many public houses or where food is served. Dogs are unwelcome in many parts of our intensively farmed countryside. We are obliged to keep the dogs we want so much virtually as prisoners, usually in great comfort but often frustrated, bored and idle. But dogs, ever adaptable, are rapidly learning to fit in.

They do not mind being out of work, although when the opportunity occurs to follow their old occupation they find it hard to resist. So you will get the gun-dog breeds anxious to wallow in whatever water they encounter, the Collie-crosses that compulsively round up anything moving – from children to motor cars – and both these activities can be dangerous. The in-born instinct to chase, to dig, to fight, or to bid for leadership of the household pack, can rise to the surface at inappropriate times and can bring the dog to some extent into conflict with its owners, but as a reader of this book you can absorb our tactics and you can always win.

Every new puppy has to learn to fit into the home to which it is taken, to fit in with the ways of the new owners and to be, to a large extent, what they want the dog to be. We can show you how to help your puppy to adapt and to achieve a happy dog/owner relationship.

2

THE PACK CONCEPT

In order to 'manage' your puppy properly it is important to understand the nature of dogs, the way they think and communicate both with humans and with other dogs. Dogs in the wild are essentially pack animals. The pack works together to find and kill food, to protect each other by warning of the approach of an enemy. Pack members will bring up each other's young and to a certain extent they will look after the sick and the weak. Their strength is that of a group working for the benefit of the whole. This group strength still survives in hunting packs of foxhounds and beagles which have a communal brain and a communal ability but often not too much individual intellect.

The survival of the wild dog pack depends on a structure of command with one male (the alpha male) and one female (the alpha female) taking dominant leadership roles and the rest of the pack establishing themselves in descending order of status, each subordinate to the ones above in the pack. The wild dog pack utilises this ranking order when hunting, fighting and most especially when feeding.

Continual challenges for leadership are made, just as in human society. While the pack leaders are young and strong their dominant role is maintained, but when overtaken by age and infirmity the pack leader would either be killed in a fight or would be demoted by a challenger.

Where several dogs are kept together in a domestic situation, the elderly pack leader may seem to withdraw in old age and will allow another strong character to take over, but often the older dog will suddenly reassert its authority and mount a challenge to the usurper. Not infrequently the pack leader is a bitch and a male dog in the domestic pack may be low down in the social order, although being a strong guard dog for the premises. Some domestic pack members are not ambitious and never seek to raise their status; others will spend their lives trying to improve their position by constantly seeking confrontation with the pack leader.

Every litter born to every bitch is essentially a dog pack from the time of birth. At first dominance is by strength only, the more virile puppies seeking out and holding on to the most productive teats, but as the puppies gain ability, the guile, courage, agility and a spirit of adventure begin to show in the potential pack leader.

The middle ranks follow with middling ability and there are always placid unambitious individuals, and always an underdog, shy, retiring, perhaps bullied by the others from as young as three weeks old. All the puppies, even the most pushy ones, are subordinate to their mother. Even if she is herself a low ranking dog in a kennel situation, she assumes the place of pack leader to her puppies. From the time of the first days after their birth, it is with some reluctance that she leaves them for even a few minutes. The breeder should ensure that the bitch and puppies are kept in a secluded place at this time, because if the bitch feels vulnerable, this can be communicated to the puppies and make them nervous. The bitch fears attack from other dogs, and perhaps cats, but she also resents visits from strange people; the most domesticated pet becomes close to the primitive dog at this time and her primary need is to keep her litter a secret so that they cannot be killed by predators. It is not unknown for other bitches to kill a litter, so there is still adequate reason for the bitch's behaviour.

Gradually, the bitch relaxes protection of the puppies until at about three weeks after the birth, they come to the beginning of the socialisation period when the litter should be brought out of seclusion and given every opportunity to see people and hear household noises, because it is at this time that they begin to adjust to the human world in which they have to live, although the maximum socialisation period does not begin until the puppies are six weeks old.

Orphan puppies which have been bottle reared lack the schooling which teaches them to behave properly with other dogs. This may not matter if they are always to live protected pet lives, but it is important in big breeds or in dogs which you hope will take part in activities with other dogs. Orphan puppies may lack the urge to mate with their own kind; they will be excessively people-orientated and so will make excellent pets, but they may be desperately unhappy and stressed if put alongside other dogs in a boarding kennel.

When choosing a puppy from a litter to be a family pet it may be unwise to decide upon the most pushy puppy, the one first to leave the nest to clamour for human attention. This pup has the potential for becoming a dominant dog, constantly making a challenge for superiority and so may become difficult to manage. Neither should you choose the backward, shy, puppy which is reluctant to leave the nest. The middle-ranking puppies generally have the best qualities to become members of your family.

The attitude of the bitch to her puppies is the keynote of your plan for dog management. As the puppies pass from the almost totally helpless, blind, deaf state in which they were born to seeing, hearing, running and barking animals at 3–4 weeks old, the bitch begins to teach the puppies the rules for life with her. Still the kind and loving mother, she very definitely indicates that there are some things she will not tolerate. It may be stealing her food, biting her ears, or using her head to play 'climbing Everest' when she and the rest of the litter want to sleep. When a puppy is annoying the bitch she acts instantly ... either by picking it up by the scruff of the neck, or by snapping at the air close to its ear, perhaps with a little rumbly growl as a first warning. The puppy, taken by surprise, will be startled and may scream, but it is unlikely to be physically hurt. The puppy usually runs, or crawls away to think the situation over ... and whether it runs or crawls may be a pointer to its future character. It may approach and repeat the annoying behaviour, and the 'bitch treatment' will be repeated as often as it takes to bring home to the puppy 'the action you are doing is against my rules and I AM IN CHARGE HERE.'

When the puppy returns to the bitch in a different frame of mind, the puppy is lovingly received, washed and comforted.

No grudges are born and there is no nagging. The reprimand is applied as the offending act is being committed not afterwards when the puppy has forgotten what it did.

The time span between an offence being committed by the dog and a reprimand being given must, throughout the dog's life, be absolutely immediate. A dog learns either by being caught in the act or by being reprimanded when the intention to transgress is obvious. Thus, when you see the dog approaching an armchair with a view to curling up in it, you can effectively say NO! at that instant and you will reinforce in the dog's mind that the armchair is forbidden territory. If you come across the dog asleep in the armchair, it is better to ignore that incident but to remind yourself to make the chair inaccessible in the future.

In the litter pack the bitch makes her displeasure apparent at once, but forgiveness and restitution of care and soothing attention are restored as soon as the puppy's attitude alters. This is the right treatment for the very young dog although later on it may be suitable deliberately to ignore an older puppy for a while to reinforce the notion that bad behaviour results in being an outcast from the pack.

Copy the bitch in managing your puppy when it is young and you will be going in the right direction, but managing a puppy in the bitch's style means that you must be constantly with the puppy, and observing its actions during the early weeks in your home. You cannot teach a puppy acceptable behaviour from a distance. *You cannot expect a puppy to learn the routine of housetraining and other acceptable behaviour patterns if there is no-one present to teach the lessons and to correct errors as they occur.*

The Puppy Pack

As we have seen, puppies get the first taste of the world from their mother, so if she is nervous and harassed, the puppies will pick up this message. In most cases the quality of fear is a learned behaviour and it can be acquired very early in life. Puppies need to begin the socialisation process at around three weeks old and it is being increasingly recognised that puppies are best reared in the house, and not in kennel accommodation.

While the breeder must always watch for a risk of infection with the virus diseases such as distemper, canine parvovirus infection and kennel cough, a compromise must be made so that the puppies get as wide an experience of the household world and human beings as possible before they leave for their new homes at seven to eight weeks old. If puppies are left in a kennel with only other dogs around, they grow up unfriendly and easily frightened, unlike a litter which has been exposed to a reasonable amount of household noise, to handling and human touch and a wide variety of body smells.

When a group of puppies begins to play together, domination comes from the puppies which are largest and have most weight. There is a good deal of play fighting which can escalate to displays of real temper from the smaller individuals with leadership ambitions but at this stage lacking the physical capability to win. While fighting, the puppies learn how far they can go and what amount of pain they can inflict before the enemy turns upon them. They learn to control biting and keep play within bounds, all very useful lessons for later life.

Puppies at play should be watched by the breeder, and they should always be under observation at feeding time, so that access to the food dish and opportunity to have possession of a toy can be manipulated so that all puppies who want to participate have an equal chance. Otherwise, the strong-willed but physically smaller puppy, often the leading bitch, can become conditioned to be over-aggressive. Puppies should not have a struggle to survive in any sense of the word, as over-development of the competitive side of their nature can spoil their suitability as a pet.

It follows that the ideal breeder should be at home, with the puppies for the whole day; the parents of the puppies should be of good equable temperament, also used to living in the house and taking part in family life; that the puppies should be raised in the house, so that they have experience of normal house noises. Puppies must be spoken to often, so that they learn to respond to the human voice; they must be regularly and well fed, receive the veterinary attention they need, and they must be gently handled.

It is obviously not possible to have a litter of puppies running

Fig. 1. Puppy play-pen apparatus.

Apparatus in puppy play-pen to give the opportunity to learn skills and to familiarise with objects. Also the opportunity for communal play which is more constructive than tormenting each other. Dominant puppy climbing out.

A Box with several holes to climb through
B Trapeze
C Apple and orange peel, very exciting when first given
D Bucket
E Rope
F Suspended ring
G Tree branch, bark removed
H Soft ball on string
I Fun with an old duster

free all over the house, so you will normally find them confined in an enclosure. The run they are enclosed in must be large enough to allow the puppies to get well away from their bed to be clean . . . puppies raised in too small a space will be harder to housetrain. A large litter, of eight or more puppies will need two runs, so that the larger male puppies do not persecute the smaller ones. Ideally constructive toys are provided so that the puppies can develop bodily skills.

Puppies must never be short of food or drink. Sometimes well meaning people may feel it is their duty to buy a puppy from a litter which has been neglected or suffered some deprivation. Early starvation, before the puppy is three months old, is very difficult to compensate; it has a profound effect on both the physique and the temperament. Leave the rehabilitation of such puppies to people very experienced in dog rearing and start with a puppy which has had every advantage up until selling time. Start with good material and compound it into a splendid companion dog.

The Dog – What It Is

1. A pack animal programmed to be submissive to those of higher status and to dominate those weaker than itself.
2. An animal that prefers not to be alone.
3. A dog barks and howls as a rallying call to the pack, a warning of danger, to draw attention to its own needs, or because it is 'imprisoned' and hoping for rescue.
4. A dog is a gorge eater, usually taking all food available to it in case there is none tomorrow.
5. A dog's instinct leads it to break down barriers between itself and the place it desires to be, agitation lending impetus to destruction sometimes out of all proportion to the apparent strength of the dog.
6. A dog is agile and athletic and needs to work off the energy we feed into it with diets of maximum nutrition.
7. All dogs and bitches, unless neutered, have at some time in their adult lives a desire for sexual activity. Puberty may start when dogs and bitches are about six months old but in the giant breeds it can be as late as two years old.

   Sexual impulse in males is of widely differing urgency, but there often seems to be a temporary surge at about 6–7 months old in male puppies. This may take the form of mating play with inanimate objects or with humans. This behaviour subsides quite quickly and no action need be taken other than verbal reprimand and distracting the puppy with some other activity.

It is becoming more and more common to have male dogs castrated when they are about a year old. The neutered dog is not a nuisance to visiting bitches or to humans, and it has no impetus to escape from its home to follow in-season bitches. Personal experience allows us to say that the neutered dog is just as lively, and as keen a guard to its home as the entire dog, and as castration does not involve entry to a body cavity, the owner need have no fears about this operation.

Most bitches have a very high libido for a few days during their heat period and the bitch may attempt to escape from her home to meet up with a male. The sexual urge at its height will supersede all learned behaviour so control by the owner and prevention of the opportunity to get away must be very strong at this time.

Consult your veterinary surgeon about having your dog or bitch neutered so as to remove one worry for your household.

8. It is a great mistake to allow your companion dog to mate a bitch just once to oblige a friend or to get a litter so that you can keep a puppy. Stud work is best left to professional stud dogs which have been screened for the hereditary diseases of their breed, and which know what behaviour is expected of them because they have a regular supply of bitches throughout their fertile years.

9. A dog likes comfort, warmth, signs of its owner's approval (even as little as a smiling glance). Dogs need and respond to physical touch.

10. In the absence of work, or training for work, a dog needs some activity for its brain, and indoor or outdoor constructive play, such as retrieving or finding thrown objects or jumping a mini-agility course, can be better for the dog than miles of road walking on the lead.

11. Because many breeds and crosses have had their coats developed to an extraordinary extent because we like the way they look, we must take on the task of thorough

Embarrassment.

Pack leader and submissive dog.
Start of domination routine.

Pack leader makes ritual growl
and clasps subordinate from
above.

Submissive gesture offering
neck for biting.

Anticipation of a reward.

The apprehensive expression.

Fig. 2. Facial expressions and dog body language.
Like those of people, dogs' facial expressions vary. Spend time
observing your own dog.

grooming. Ask the breeder to show you what your breed requires and the tools you may need to buy. Baths may be given as often as necessary.

12. A dog has less brain capacity than man, and the canine brain works in a different way from ours. Dogs cannot plan ahead or visualise the consequences of their actions. A dog responds to outside stimuli, particularly to smell and to incidents which happen at a regular time.

The dog has a memory, possibly stimulated by recurrence of scent or noise. There is considerable doubt as to whether a dog can feel guilt about some misdemeanour it has committed. What we term as a guilty look may be in fact a response to the owner's obvious dismay or disapproval.

13. Dogs are creatures of routine and habit and learn easily by repetition.

14. A dog communicates with other canines and humans by body postures and facial expressions (body language). He has all the time in the world to observe his owners and is thus able to interpret the tiniest expression of human body language which you may even be unaware that you make. We can communicate better with dogs if we study their body language.

3

BODY LANGUAGE: UNDERSTANDING WHAT DOGS ARE SAYING

The Dominant Dog

The Dominant dog stands upright, a line of hair on spine (the hackles) stands erect, tail up and gently wagging. This is a primeval device to make the dog look larger and more fierce, and it is caused by the upsurge of adrenaline which triggers the fight and flight syndrome.

Fig. 3. Body language.

When approached by other dogs, the dominant animal curls its lips, makes a snarling roar, neck is extended, a paw may be put on the approaching dog.

The Submissive Dog
The Submissive dog approaches the other from the side, never head on. The head is held low, body crouching, rear end high. The underdog licks head and lips of pack leader. Finally it presents back of neck (vital part) for pack leader to bite, or rolls on its back to expose the groin area. But if the submission ritual is well done, there will be no bite inflicted.

Puppies from three to nine months old *expect* to be submissive to adults, even those physically much smaller than themselves. Adult dogs may punish and reprimand puppies but they do not fight them.

Urination Rituals – Territory Marking
Both males and females urinate in the squatting position as puppies. At about nine months to one year old the male will begin urinating with raised leg, this position is more convenient for marking posts and bushes. Territory marking usually goes with the onset of adult behaviour. Bitches mark but at the squat or with one hind leg partially raised. This is usually only done when they are coming into season. Adult males mark their territory and regular walks by directing a stream of urine at certain well-defined points, probably endeavouring to blot out the mark of other dogs.

Selected shrubs in the garden will also be marked – small conifers seem to be the favourite target – and eventually they turn yellow and die. Do not plant another one in the same place! Males may also mark, usually once only, a new object or piece of furniture brought into the house.

If an unfamiliar male dog is brought into your house or garden, or a bitch is in season nearby, or even if a visitor has bitch scent on their clothes, your own male dog may shame you by urine-marking indoors. This behaviour is so instinctive in the male dog that it is unfair to be harsh with him; instead take steps to limit other dogs visiting the territory. Make sure all marking is expunged with a disinfectant especially designed to take away

Fig. 4. Dominant and submissive dogs.
　Above:　The dominant dog shows signs of aggression, legs
　　　　　straight, hackles raised, tail waving, and teeth bared.
　Below:　The submissive smile, which is accompanied by lowered
　　　　　head and body, lowered wagging tail, and may progress
　　　　　to lying on side and exposing the groin.

scent . . . your veterinary surgery can advise you.

Both dogs and bitches seem to take a lot of interest in the faeces of other animals. This habit should be stopped as much as possible to prevent the possible transmission of infection, and because 'taking an interest' can often lead to actually eating manure etc.: a very unpleasant canine habit.

Bitches can be difficult about urination away from home, if they cannot use the same type of surface they are used to; some will only use grass, others concrete. Bitches will hold their urine for up to 48 hours in such circumstances although given every opportunity to be clean. Bitches often behave in this way in boarding kennels, and it is taken as a sign of acceptance of the kennel when at last the bitch will christen her run with a big puddle.

Puppies and emotional bitches may urinate involuntarily in extreme pleasure, perhaps as a greeting; they usually grow out of this habit, which is a demonstration of submission.

Licking
Most dogs lick their feet and genitals to keep them clean. This is a natural act but it should only be allowed for a limited time. Licking is also a submissive act, but puppies will lick the mouth of a bitch to trigger a regurgitation of partly digested food. This may be the reason that puppies tend to lick children all round the face if they are allowed to. Blood and suppurative discharges are attractive to the dog and they seem impelled to lick wounds.

Sleeping Behaviour
Dogs turn in circles before lying down to flex the spine before going into a tightly curled position to conserve body heat. Only when very warm will they sleep on their sides with feet extended; when a dog is very hot it may lie on its stomach with hind feet extended to bring as much surface as possible in contact with a cool floor. A very relaxed and warm dog will lie on its back with four feet bent up. Dogs will readily assume any position for which they have been extravagantly praised or which has proved rewarding. Our puppy, Berry, looked so appealing lying on her back with feet in the air that we were impelled to pay her attention; now she slides into this pose often, very obviously keeping her eyes on us to see if it has been noticed.

Dogs dream, as people do. They give muffled barks and kick their legs while still deeply asleep.

Vocal Behaviour

Dogs can vary their bark according to what they want to convey. Most dogs bark at doorbells but seldom at telephones. This may be because the owners are not apprehensive of a telephone call. Howling is regarded by many people as a bad omen but to the dog it is just a sound that carries better than a bark, and howling is always done standing or sitting, never on the move, as barking may be. The growl and snarl are warnings of further action to come, unless the adversary gives in. It may be only bluff on the dog's part, but it is up to the owner to see that a dog never ends a growling session as a winner. Some dogs communicate with a grunt-growl noise; be sure which your dog is doing.

Tail wagging

This usually means pleasure, but waving the tail may be a sign of aggression. Tails are tucked down between legs when a dog runs away in fear, except in the greyhound-type dogs which habitually carry their tails in this position (Borzoi, Italian Greyhound).

Guarding

Some dogs, although not of guarding breed, become very possessive about their bed, toys or bones. This attitude must be broken down very early, as the owner must be superior to the dog in every way, even to taking its possessions.

A 'biter' is not a guard dog, it is just a dangerous dog. The dog that backs away, snapping and biting through fear is showing its own incompetence at dealing with a situation.

Some dogs show extravagant guarding behaviour when in a car, perhaps because with so much glass around them they feel vulnerable to attack from all sides. Dogs of the guarding breeds should usually be friendly in puppy days; the guard dog instinct often does not show until the dog is two years old.

Stealing

Dogs have no sense of moral values. They take what they find, unless given the direct command, at the time, not to touch. Food should not be left unattended when dogs are present, it is unhygienic to say the least.

4

THE CANINE SENSES

Dogs communicate and get their information about the world by sight, hearing, body language (postures assumed by the body), but mainly by smell. The male dog has a unique sense of territory, and will, when adult, mark with urine several points around the garden and on regular walks; these appear to be sites where he perceives himself to be 'in charge'. These points are marked again frequently, certainly after any other dog has urinated on the marks he put previously, or if another dog has even passed that way.

It is believed that this urine can vary in strength and chemical content to convey to other dogs quite a lot about the 'marker', usually including its ferocity and breeding status. Bitches do not perform ritual marking except when coming into season, but some older, dominant bitches will make an attempt at leg raising while urinating . . . probably an excess of masculine component in their personality.

The scenting power of the dog is beyond our comprehension; even the short-nosed dogs can find and identify scent of which we are not even aware. Those dogs with long noses and wide nostrils, and heavy ears bringing the nose close to the ground (Bassets, Bloodhounds) have scenting ability which is almost limitless compared with the human.

The dog's own scent, emitted chiefly from glands under the tail, tells another dog about its temper, intentions and even its pack status. Scent perception makes it difficult for us to deceive or trick dogs; they recognise the clothes we wear for different activities by scent, not colour or fashion design, and they can recognise their owner in any disguise. Dogs will chew on an object just handled by their owner, this is why it is the new book or today's newspaper that gets torn and not something discarded days ago. Guard dogs seem to recognise people with bad intentions by the scent they give off, probably the sweat of fear. Puppies find their way to the bitch while they are yet blind and deaf, by scent; the bitch recognises her own newborn puppies by their scent, and will reject any others put into her nest unless the scent of her own litter is applied to them. This special litter scent must be lost or forgotten as the puppies grow up. Puppies which remain in the pack with the bitch always get special consideration from her and some continuing maternal attention even when they are completely adult, but those puppies which are sold are not recognised when they return to their ancestral home. They are usually treated as intruders by their mother.

Sight
In comparison with the complexity and versatility of the human eye the dog has a simple visual system. The dog cannot, for example, distinguish distant objects unless they are moving, and as far as we know they can only see shades of grey. A person standing against a hedge only a short distance away from a dog may be invisible to it, even if wearing bright clothes, if the wind is carrying the person's scent away.

It is wise, from the beginning of your dog's education, to combine your commands with hand signals so as to give your dog every chance to obey. Dogs with flat faces (Boxers, Pugs, Pekes) can judge distance well but are not as long-sighted as those breeds which have their eyes positioned on each side of a prominent nose (Collies, Bull Terriers). These dogs are dependant on turning the eyes and the whole head to see what is going on around them.

It is important in this context to realise that behaviour correction given by the hand, rolled up newspaper or stick may make a dog unduly fearful of any arm movement on the edge of its vision. A dog constantly on the defensive against such a weapon may feel threatened by someone making harmless expansive gestures with their arms. Some of the unexplainable attacks made by dogs upon innocent adults or children may be due to a sudden movement of this kind at the edge of the dog's visual field, especially when it is used to fearing such actions. Dominant dogs object strongly to the threat of a physical blow by someone who is not their pack leader.

Dogs also tend to feel threatened by, or show fear of, people who convey unusual messages by body language. People who are lame, or in wheelchairs, or have some other physical disability which alters their voice or their manner may engender fear in the dog, so will people carrying unusual burdens, such as a sack over the shoulder or a big rucksack piled up with equipment.

Your dog's eyesight is a very important sense, both to the dog and to you the owner. If you notice any change in the dog's eyes, such as redness, a film over the eye, or the eye kept closed against light, or if your dog seems to have difficulty in seeing in dim light, consult your veterinary surgeon at once. Some eye defects in the popular breeds are inherited. The British Veterinary Association in conjunction with the Kennel Club run schemes for the screening of such defects. Your veterinary surgery will have the details.

Hearing
The ear of the dog is much more acute and more discerning than our own. Dogs can hear sounds on a much higher register, so the so-called silent whistle can be used in training them.

Those breeds with pricked up, wide open ears (German Shepherd Dog, Pharaoh Hound) can suffer acutely if confined in a household where someone plays the trumpet or where the TV sound or stereo is always turned up to full strength.

Companion dogs have to cope with a deluge of sound which does not concern them and yet they can pick up a familiar word used in conversation as much as 25 yards away. Their own names are perhaps the words they are most attuned to, for they are used to hearing their name said sharply, in anger or in a caressing voice. Other words are only significant when used in the appropriate tone, as praise or admonishment.

Some very high pitched sounds seem to give dogs actual pain, and they will show fear or resentment, according to their nature, at some food mixers, or circular saws, even when they are familiar with the apparatus.

Unfamiliar noises are startling or alarming to dogs, and owners must always be aware that the dog may react badly, for instance, to children who scream while playing; to baby noises; even to people singing if it is not a normal activity in the dog's household. The noise made will be much more intense to the dog.

The location of a sound in open countryside seems difficult for dogs and they may need extra sight or scent clues to find a person calling them from a distance. Get your dog used to a combination of sign and sound commands.

Very precise identification of sounds important to the dog is possible, for instance the sound of their own food bowl is distinguished from that of other cooking utensils, and they soon learn to pick out the engine sound of their owner's car. It may be useful to remember that when you are moving house or decorating and rooms are empty of furniture, every sound echoes in an unfamiliar way and your dog may become more care-seeking for this reason.

Touch

A dog's natural response to being touched by strange hands is to recoil and be on the defensive or very submissive, according to type, but the touch of an experienced veterinary surgeon or dog handler is seldom resented, because these people approach the dog in the right way. It is foolish and dangerous to touch a strange dog of a guard breed without having permission from the owner to do so. Once accepted, touching by stroking can be a very effective rewarding action for a dog, and some smooth-coated dogs seem to receive positive comfort by being in body contact with other dogs or humans . . . they need to lie close together, and with other dogs, will pile on top of one another.

It has been observed that when dogs are stimulated by sound, sight and touch at the same time, the response to touch will dominate, so it may be unproductive to try to condition a dog to react to words while touching. But we teach SIT with word and touch very successfully.

If a dog looks aggressive and dominant never try to stroke it from above; your hand may appear as a threat. Offer the back of your hand to the dog to sniff . . . on the principle that your scent

Fig. 5. A pat on the head.
What a pat on the head looks like to a dog. See how threatening the human hand appears.

will convey your good intentions, and then, if reaction is favourable, stroke the dog low down on its body.

Reflexes

As well as the need to understand its place in the pack the puppy must also learn to make the appropriate response to an outside stimulus if it is to survive. In essence, this is done by trial and error, and the dog learns by getting a pleasurable or unpleasurable reaction following a specific activity. The puppy has, by the time it is twelve weeks old, already acquired a set of reflex behaviours, superimposed on inborn reflexes like sucking and feeding, urine marking and territory guarding, and maternal behaviour in the bitches. Not all dogs have inborn reflexes to the same degree; occasionally bitches lack maternal instinct, for instance.

Summary

1. Dogs depend extensively on their sense of smell. Sniffing, for a dog, is equal to our reading a newspaper; dogs get all their information from reading the scent of other animals and people.

    Dogs can scent fear in people and this can make them aggressive.
2. Dogs see moving objects more easily than stationary ones. Sudden movements by strangers alarm dogs.
3. A dog's hearing is much more acute than our own. Loud noises can cause discomfort to a dog's sensitive ears.
4. Some dogs resent being touched by strangers. Never attempt to touch a dog by bringing your hand down from above its head, and always avoid staring directly into an unfamiliar dog's eyes.

Section II

THE DOG IN YOUR HOME

5

THE DOG'S NEEDS

Before you make any moves at all to choose a dog for your family, it is important to visualise what its life will be with you, not only on lovely sunny mornings but in the depths of winter when the days for exercising are very short. The place where you intend to take your dog for day-to-day exercise is an important consideration. If you have to use a public park, a very large dog or a hound type dog, prone to chase other furry creatures, may not be suitable. While large dogs do not necessarily mean to injure the small, they are inclined to show domination particularly if the small dog challenges them, as some small breeds are very inclined to do, and may hurt them unintentionally. While such a confrontation would, in the vast majority of cases, end amicably if the dogs were left alone, the presence of worried, perhaps screaming owners complicates and distorts the situation, and inevitably gets the larger dog a bad reputation which is often quite undeserved.

Sad though it may be to deny many worthy people the pleasure of dog ownership, we feel that it is not a good plan to acquire a dog unless you can allow it some free choice of access to the outside world; every dog needs a tiny garden, a paved patio or even a balcony to which it can come and go at will. However dutiful you may be about taking the dog out a minimum of four times a day, it seems to impose too much restriction on a dog if it can never choose for itself whether to be outside or not, can never potter about looking for the things dogs look for, free of human interference.

If you are able to allow your dog free access to a garden, then the garden must be fenced, to a height suitable to the breed. Many big dogs can jump and scramble over six feet easily and if there is any attraction in neighbouring gardens, they will do so directly your eye is off them. It is anti-social to let any dog wander off your own property besides putting your dog at risk.

It is a very good idea to get the fencing done before you get the puppy, right up to the maximum height which will be needed, rather than wait until the dog has cleared the existing fence once. Any successful action of this kind is counter-productive to keeping the dog within bounds. The dog, having been rewarded by freedom, will try again and again to jump out.

Gates should have secure fastenings, high up, but easy for all the family to use, and it is preferable if the back garden can be securely cut off from any road with motor traffic. Dogs, like children, seem attracted to get to places which afford them the greatest danger, but you cannot reason with a puppy as you could with a child.

Unsupervised dogs, particularly those which have just dashed out of an open door or gap in the hedge, have no road sense at all. They are the cause of many road accidents and their owners are liable for the damage caused to the car and the occupants.

Puppies and young dogs, or newly acquired adult dogs, do not do well where all members of the family are away for many hours of the day. Dogs get lonely and bored, and consequently noisy and destructive, and it is impossible to teach a puppy good behaviour unless there is someone present to correct it when it does wrong, or praise it when it does well. When dogs are alerted by a caller at the house, many will continue to bark for hours unless checked and there will be, quite justly, complaints by the neighbours. A mature dog may be left safely for four to five hours sometimes but even this should not be on a regular basis.

As a dog breeder I am often asked to let a puppy go to someone who works 'mornings only'. I find this situation unacceptable since in the very nature of things the dog will not be exercised enough to be tired before the family leaves for work in the morning. All the alerting noises of tradesmen happen in the morning too, and a working session of four hours can often mean a six-hour stretch away from home by the time the shopping is done as well. 'Afternoons only' is a better proposition, but neither is ideal.

Some employers will allow well behaved dogs to accompany staff to work (the guard dog element can be a persuasive factor) and it may be possible to allow the dog to remain in your car part of the day, but remember how easily a stationary car heats up in summer and be sure to park in the shade and allow plenty of ventilation.

Your working day will inevitably be broken up by the need to attend to the dog, but this is only one example of the 'sacrifices' you will have to make if you take a dog into your family as a dependant to be cared for and planned for.

You may feel that taking on an older dog may be easier, but dogs looking for second or third owners usually have some behaviour or personality fault which has caused them to be unwanted by the original owners. You may not find out the snags until a crisis occurs. Alternatively, you may be lucky in being able to take on a well-loved pet which the previous owners cannot keep for some viable reason. In taking on an adult dog it is all the more necessary not to leave it alone for any length of time until you thoroughly understand the way it reacts and until the dog feels really secure in your home. Newly acquired adult dogs are very easily lost when off the lead, either because they become disorientated, do not recognise you as their owner, or because they are attempting to return to their first home. Even if the dog is good at 'come when called' in the garden, do not rely on your control over it outside the home until two or three months have passed.

The Indoor Kennel

One purchase which may seem expensive at first but which will be invaluable for the whole of your dog's life is an indoor kennel, also known as a 'crate'. This is essentially a folding box made out of wire mesh comprising sides, lid, floor and door, and can be erected within minutes anywhere you want it to be. The 'crate' can be in the kitchen when you are cooking, in the sitting-room when you have visitors, in the garden, in the bedroom when there is the need. The crate can go on holiday

Fig. 6. The indoor kennel or crate.
Wire cages for enclosing the pup for short periods. They soon become a favourite 'home' and can be collapsed into a flat package for storage or removal.

with you, reassuring your hosts that your dog will be under control at all times.

The great advantage of the crate is that the dog does not feel enclosed. He can be where the action is and see everything that is happening and yet feel perfectly safe. You can leave the door open to allow the crate to be the dog's own preferred resting place, or you can shut the door to keep the dog perfectly safe.

Buy the size which will suit your dog when he is adult, and pad it with blankets to make it cosy enough for a puppy. Specially adapted crates can also be bought to fit into most popular cars.

6

CHOOSING A DOG

Adoption Of Older Dogs
The choice here may be between a dog from a general rescue organisation or a pedigree breed specialist rescue service, or a dog or bitch surplus to showing or breeding requirements from a pedigree breeder's kennel.

Rescued Dogs
Dogs which have been in rescue homes for several weeks may have become conditioned to jumping and biting at the wire, to be constant barkers for attention and to be plotting their escape from prolonged confinement in kennels.

Recently, one such rescue organisation, the Blue Cross, has employed a canine behaviour consultant to assess the behaviour of rescued dogs, both in their attitude towards people and their general behaviour. The dogs then receive rehabilitation training which makes them suitable to join family homes. Rather than choosing a dog from a rescue kennel, it is more common nowadays to be 'prescribed' a particular dog by a member of staff who knows the dog and its attributes well. Do not resent this, as it is intended to help you to give a home to the dog which will best suit you and your situation.

A Puppy: Mongrel, Crossbred or Pedigreed?
Mongrel
Mongrel litters are seldom deliberately bred, they are nature's accidents and so it follows that the litter is unlikely to have had as much care, conditioning and knowledge behind it as the pedigree litter.

The product of several generations of wanderers, as most mongrel litters are, is unlikely to be easy to keep at home, and you will not know what 'ingredients' you have in your puppy. Knowing the in-bred character traits is a great help in managing your puppy.

Crossbreds

Crossbreds, that is the product of two known, pedigreed dogs, are sometimes known as 'Kennel Maid's accidents'. The inadvertent pairing of dog and bitch does happen in the best run kennels and the result may be an unorthodox but well-reared puppy, provided the natures of the two parents are compatible. Pairings between varieties of gun-dog or Collie cross gun-dogs seem to work well. In mongrel and crossbred matings the puppies are often larger than the parents, and the coat tends to be smooth more often than rough, and seldom silky. It is also interesting that where short faces are paired with long, the short face is entirely lost in the first generation and not regained . . . you never see a pug-faced mongrel and Boxer crosses are always long nosed but tend to have Boxer body shape.

Your reception will not be cordial if you telephone your local kennel asking if they have any 'accidents' to dispose of . . . they are likely to deny that any such thing could ever happen. You get to hear of these puppies by word of mouth or by advertisements in the local press. Do not buy a crossbred unless you see the puppies with their mother; you must be sure of at least half of the partnership and preferably both halves.

Pedigreed Dogs

There are more than 140 separate breeds of pedigreed dogs, so there is bound to be one which suits your lifestyle and your inclination, but as with marriage, you will be unwise to choose entirely by looks. The dog you are buying should be part of your family for about ten years at least, and you will have in that time to spend a lot of money and a lot of care and affection upon it, so it makes sense to take plenty of time and trouble to choose your dog, and never to buy on impulse.

Many families are stampeded into buying a puppy because

they have promised the children to get one and once the intention is declared, the children will not wait. The best advice is to keep your intentions secret while you do the preliminary exploration and even the final choosing; this is an area where adults should have the final word. There is nothing more embarrassing than to have to drag children away from a kennel as they wail 'Why won't you buy a puppy from that lady, Daddeeee . . .?'

It is important to remember that dogs glorified by exposure on advertisements, in cartoons and in television appearances are not necessarily, or even likely to be, as accommodating and adaptable as they seem. The Old English Sheepdog and the Basset Hound are two breeds that come to mind as having been exploited shamefully in this way and a great many families have been very disappointed when they got these dogs into their homes. We watch the Border Collies at Sheepdog Trials with great admiration, but these dogs are under strong domination by the handlers, and they are given long days at work which curbs their energy. In idleness, the Border Collie can become hysterical, and a *sheep chaser*. This breed is quick to learn but it must do something with the skill it acquires, either the work for which it was bred, or else have the mental stimulus of competing in Obedience Trials.

Coat Type
All dogs have to get rid of their dead hair coat in some way – most shed hair, but the Poodle and Bedlington have theirs cut off, rather expensively, at six-weekly intervals. These last two breeds may be suitable, however, for asthmatic patients allergic to ordinary dog hair. Dogs used to be said to moult twice a year, but since we have taken many heavy-coated dogs to live in our centrally heated houses, they lose their hair all the year round. Surprisingly, really long hair can be easier to remove from carpets than the hair from short-coated dogs which can become imbedded in fabric.

If you buy a long-haired dog, grooming must be done every day, in order to keep the underlying skin healthy and to keep the dog acceptable in your home . . . a matted coat is a degradation to the dog and renders it unsuitable to be in the house. One factor to consider is where the grooming is to be done. You will not want to brush the dog and have the debris flying about your living quarters. Dogs with corded coats (the Puli and the Komondor) can take the place of handicraft work for their owners: you twirl the hair into cords while watching television!

Dogs with soft woolly undercoats (German Shepherds, Corgis) can be a real problem at some times of the year when the coat comes out in handfuls. It is best to take the dog into the garden and strip out as much as possible.

Size

The next choice lies between large, medium or small dog, a weight range between about 1.8kg (4 lbs) in the Chihuahua, and 63–68kg (140–150 lbs) in the Newfoundland, and something for all tastes in between.

Large dogs fill a very different role in the family from that of the tiny pet, which is essentially a cuddle-object, a comforter, an amusement, or a little status symbol. There is always an ego-boost for the person who can 'do what they like' with a dog which weighs as much or more than many humans; the affection of such a powerful creature does confer a special blessing. Big dogs have shoulders to cry on and sides you can slap, and even those not specially bred for guard tendencies look forbidding enough to the prospective intruder. Not all large dogs are greedy for exercise, some, like the Mastiff, are quite lethargic; some, like the Wolfhound, will curl down into quite a small space, but others, notably Setters and Dalmatians, must have rooms big enough for them to turn around without swishing all the things off the coffee table with their tails. You can get a St Bernard into a tiny car, but it feels uncomfortable and looks rather silly, and big dogs do like to retain their dignity.

In describing so many breeds in a few words it is inevitable that some injustice will be done by too much generalisation, but it is as well to be aware of the characteristics of some of the most popular breeds because this should influence your choice quite profoundly. Remember that large dogs will need the most expensive size in collars, beds, and feeding bowls; that their veterinary bills will in most cases be larger, as larger doses of drugs are used, and they require larger accommodation at boarding kennels, and eat more.

On the other hand, there are expenses which do not vary with breed; preventative vaccinations cost the same for the tiny or the largest dog; premiums for third party insurance and to cover veterinary treatment are the same, and a railway ticket for a dog accompanying a passenger is charged at identical rate for a Beagle or a St Bernard.

The smallest dogs can be too fragile for family life, very fine bones are easily broken and joints may be displaced in a well-meant rough and tumble. Papillons, Chihuahuas, Yorkies and Toy Poodles suit adult homes best, and are ideal for those who must travel by public transport, as they are easy to carry on buses, and will travel free on trains provided they are in a container carried by the passenger.

Popular Breeds
The Hound Breeds
The Hound breeds are conditioned to hunt, by sight or by scent, and the compulsion to do so can make them take every opportunity to escape from house and garden, or from control when on a walk. Afghans and Salukis, hounds which hunt by sight, can almost never be let off the lead in open country, as even their greatest devotees have to admit that these hounds seldom obey a command when running free. Basenjis are mischievous, may climb on top of your highest cupboard, but they are fun to own. While not having the bark of other dogs, they do have a yodel, and are by no means silent. Dachshunds were taught to bark while they were underground, flushing fox and badger out of their lairs. This breed still has the persistent loud bark and they are also great diggers, so you will have to bury your boundary fence deep into the ground. Beagles are the ideal size and shape for companion dogs and they have lovely temperament but they will escape if they get the chance.

Best companion material among the hounds:
Finnish Spitz and Whippets.

Absolutely unsuitable for novice owners:
Ex-pack Foxhounds, Otterhounds, Bloodhounds, Borzois.
Afghans and Salukis unless you have several acres of fenced
ground available.

Gun-dogs

Gun-dogs usually have good temperament and mix happily with
other dogs, but they are capable of working all day in bad
weather, and confinement is therefore frustrating and can cause
a deterioration in temperament. Golden Retrievers and Labradors are among the kindest dogs known. They make splendid
companions for children as they will retrieve and play hide and
seek endlessly. Both these breeds are used extensively as Guide
Dogs for the Blind, a tribute to their ability to take direction and
training, but they must have mental and physical activity every
day. All the Setters are lively, high-spirited dogs, they remain
puppyish for a long time.

The Weimaraner's unique silver-grey colouring makes it
very attractive, but temperament is not as easy as in other
gun-dogs, and they need work.

The Cocker Spaniel is now rarely used as a gun-dog and
over-popularity immediately post-World War II contributed to
a deterioration in temperament in the black and the red colouring. The coats of the blacks need regular trimming. English and
Welsh Springer Spaniels have good temperament which can be
spoilt by a too restrictive life. The untrained gun-dog is always
liable to take off after game on a country walk, often with
disastrous results.

Best companion dog material:
The Labrador, Golden Retriever and the Pointer.

Terriers

Terriers were bred to hunt rodents; their special attributes are
keenness, persistence and quick snapping jaws. Temperaments
are good: not too dependent on owner company and with the
ability to keep busy on their own in the garden. The snatching
habit of the terriers may make them unsuitable where there are
toddler-age children in the family.

Most terriers need professional stripping, by terrier special-ists, twice a year to keep them in good shape, the Border Terrier being an exception.

Bull Terriers and Staffordshire Bull Terriers are the result of 18th and 19th century crosses to provide keen determined dogs for bull baiting and fighting. Both breeds still enjoy a good scrap but are wonderfully devoted family pets and are trustworthy with children. They are not quite so dependent on human com-pany as the proper Bull breeds, having a modification of terrier self-reliance.

Good companion dog material:
Border Terrier, Cairn Terrier, Staffordshire Bull Terrier.

Shepherding Dogs
The German Shepherd Dog (Alsatian) is the world's most popular dog, and rightly so. The many different duties it performs as Guide Dog, and with the police and the armed forces of the world are a tribute to this dog's versatility, but they may be shy and therefore untrustworthy. It has a very strong guarding instinct which is easily misdirected and this dog must have sensible, but never harsh, handling. It is essential to take veterinary advice before buying a German Shepherd because they can have a number of hereditary problems. The Briard is a French herding dog, shaggy coated, very good natured and rapidly becoming popular. Of the Collies, the Bearded Collie is the most suitable family dog; Shetland Sheepdogs can be shy and have a high-pitched bark; Rough Collies (Lassie-dogs) may resent visitors to the family. The Border Collie excels at Obedience work. Many people will have admired their ability in sheep herding competitions but may have failed to observe that the dogs are under very strong dominance by their handlers. These dogs, taken so recently from a working background, must have something to do in their day. All sheep herding dogs may, if untrained, become *sheep chasers*.

Best companion dog material:
Bearded Collie, Briard.

Not for novices:
Old English Sheepdog (because of grooming problems).

The Guarding Breeds

These are power-packed dogs, capable of inflicting serious injury on an intruder or anyone making an attack upon their owner, but they are very agreeable and tolerant within the family. Because a guard dog may sometimes misinterpret a caller's intention, all guarding breeds must be kept under strict supervision and they must respond to command instantly. Most guarding breeds tend to want to dominate other dogs, so they are not suitable to exercise off the lead in public parks. The European man-made breeds of the 19th century figure prominently among the modern guard dogs; the Doberman, Boxer, Rottweiler and Giant Schnauzer are examples.

Boxers are the most exuberant and boisterous of the guarding breeds; they are great playmates for older children and well liked by publicans and hotel keepers . . . the Boxer loves people as long as people are doing the right things. Bred, like the Rottweiler, to be a personal guard and companion, these dogs expect to be with people constantly and they are very poor 'yard guards', doing their best work from an armchair in the hall. Dobermans are more elegant to look at, but sharper in their work, being used by some police forces. Bull Mastiffs are placid, Mastiffs even more so, except when guarding ability is needed.

None of these dogs needs training to guard, the instinct is there and will come to the surface when needed however soft your dog may appear in daily life. It is extremely dangerous to encourage any of these breeds to show aggression, even as a joke.

Best companion dog material for family wanting a guarding dog:
Boxer (for laughs), Doberman (for serious deterrent).

Toy Breeds

Among the Toy Dogs there are miniature versions of many of the large breeds. The Cavalier King Charles Spaniel is the largest of the breeds termed 'Toy'. They have some of the hunting attributes of the spaniel but most of the breed are submissive in character, unassuming with other dogs and easy to board as they settle with anyone who is kind to them. Some owners may find the modern Cavalier a little lacking in character. The Yorkshire Terrier is still a superb ratter when not hampered by excess coat. Pugs and Pekes need to keep their cool, both in fights with other dogs and in the conditions in which they live. Their breathing apparatus is soon overtaxed in warm weather and stuffy rooms.

Chihuahuas are not very friendly to visitors and are not children's dogs.

Best companion dog material in small package:
Tibetan Spaniel (Peke-like but more athletic), the Griffon (sporty), and the larger Poodles and poodle-cross terriers.

Other Breeds

The Bernese Mountain Dog, adept at pulling carts, makes a genial but large companion for children. Welsh Corgis were bred to herd and drive cattle by nipping the heels of the laggards. Essentially a working farm dog, they were not kept as pets until taken up by the Royal family in the late 1930s. Corgis still have to be shown from a very early age that biting is against the rules.

Bulldogs are slow movers, obstinate, not very long lived, but cheerful and good tempered. As they walk at a slow amble, they are very well suited to adults with the same inclinations. French Bulldogs are smaller, lively and affectionate and, like the Boston Terrier, have a lot of the bull-breed attributes in a small package. They are highly recommended.

The Tibetan dogs – Shih Tzu, Tibetan Terrier, Lhasa Apsos and Tibetan Spaniel – have shrill penetrating voices; they were alleged to bark a warning of approaching travellers from the ramparts of the monasteries. The first three Tibetan breeds require a lot of grooming. Schipperkes and Keeshonds are also 'warning' dogs but not guards, very agreeable as pets.

Poodles are among the most versatile of all companion dogs, much more down to earth than their show appearances would indicate.

(Many apologies to all the breeds there was not room to mention!)

Inherited Defects

Some of the most popular breeds which make good companion dog material have some inherited physical defects, only seen as the dog gets older. Breeders are in the main working very hard to eliminate disease from their stock, but it is essential to get veterinary advice before you buy a German Shepherd Dog, Miniature or Toy Poodle, Labrador, Golden Retriever or a Cocker Spaniel.

Always buy direct from the breeder where you can see the mother with her litter, and possibly some other related dogs as well. If choosing a large breed, it is a great advantage to see some adolescent dogs, rough and boisterous, and not to make your decision only on the basis of the quiet maternal bitch and little puppies. Your own summing up of the breeder's attitude, the surroundings in which the puppies are being reared, and the advice and friendship of the breeder who takes continuing interest in the puppies after sale is of inestimable benefit to you. None of these advantages will be yours if you buy from a pet shop, or a dealer where puppies are bought in from a variety of sources. Veterinary surgeons have declared that it is a handicap affecting physical and mental health for a puppy to move homes more than once before twelve weeks of age.

All dogs are expensive to rear well; you pay not only for the puppy but for all the care given to the mother before the birth and the fee paid for the use of the stud dog.

Exotic and rare breeds newly imported to this country obviously cost more and those where the bitches have trouble giving birth, for instance Bulldogs are always expensive; breeds which have large litters (Irish Setters, Labradors) come much cheaper than tiny Yorkshire Terriers – that breed is almost international currency these days.

The Purchase

It makes sense to buy your puppy as close to your home as possible. You will have all the benefit of keeping in touch with the breeder and the puppy will have only a short journey to your home. Your local veterinary surgeon may be able to advise you about litters which are due; in any case, it is wise to contact a veterinary practice before you make the purchase. Most veterinary surgeons will advise prospective owners about the suitability of the breed it is proposed to get, and this service is usually free of charge. If you want the vet to examine the puppy for fitness, this will command a fee but it will be money well spent. If there should be anything drastically wrong with the puppy you have chosen, it is much better to know at once, before you have got so fond of the little dog that you feel obliged to keep it. You could let yourself in for a trying time, both financially and emotionally, if you take on an ailing puppy.

You will find advertisements of puppies for sale in the two weekly papers, *Dog World* and *Our Dogs*, as well as in the monthly journals *Your Dog*, *Dogs Monthly* and *Dogs Today*. The Kennel Club will let you have a list of breeders with puppies for sale and The Pet Plan Insurance Group's Puppyline service will send lists of puppies for sale which are updated daily (see Appendix for details).

Responsible breeders do not have puppies available all the time. Many of the people who supply the best companion stock breed only occasionally, when they have compiled a waiting list for puppies. More and more breeders are feeling that it is unethical to have litters of puppies available to sell to impulse buyers, so when you do locate a litter you may find they are all booked. Disappointing though this may be at the time, it augurs well for the puppy that you will buy from such a breeder in the future, for a puppy programmed to be a companion dog from the start is what you are looking for. As litters do not always provide the sexes in the ratio required, you may find some puppies unbooked, but then your choice is limited.

It is difficult to get puppy buyers to look beyond the skin, and buyers frequently ask for a 'red dog with one white sock just like our old Kim' . . . but surely it was character that made Kim so beloved and not really his overcoat? The pick of the litter is usually taken to mean the puppy with all features corresponding as far as is possible in one so young, with the Kennel Club standard for the breed. Choosing a companion by evaluation of temperament allows you to consider the whole litter, including mismarked puppies.

Family Involvement

It is important, before making any more progress with your plans, to be sure that everyone in the family and even those people who work in your house and garden really want a puppy and will follow out your plan for management. Just one person who feels aggravated or resentful can ruin your scheme and one person over-indulgent or too sympathetic can do just as much harm. People play out a lot of their own resentments and spites via the family dog, and this is especially true where the new puppy causes some employee more work and trouble.

A point for very close consideration is the attitude of the women of the family: are they being honest and truthful about their wish to have a dog? As a generalisation, women like to please their men and children, and will loyally declare that they do indeed long for a dog about the place. Unfortunately, some dogs are unsuccessful pets because the women in the home had not pictured just how much more housework the dog would make, or how much the new puppy would curb their freedom. Care of the dog so often devolves on the one at home all day and a desire to please the rest of the family cannot always be maintained when coping with the actuality of the dog underfoot.

In order to manage the puppy skilfully, it must be *wanted* by *all* the family, and they must *all* feel equal goodwill towards it. The dog that is shut out all day in order to save pawmarks on the kitchen floor, or the dog that is unreasonably chastised when it cannot associate punishment with the deed, may grow into a nervous animal, and only then will you realise that someone has not been following the family's plan for its management.

The confident, happy dog, which feels that the world is a reliable place where human behaviour is consistent, is the dog which will bring you compliments everywhere.

Sometimes parents are motivated to get a dog because one of their children has developed an unreasonable fear of dogs. It is better to break down the phobia by periodic association with a reliable, co-operative older dog before you introduce a dog or puppy into your own household. A dog may be adversely affected by a show of fear; it would be reasonable to expect a puppy to run after a child which runs away from it, but if the child is running in fear, the puppy will have to be restrained. A dominant puppy in such a situation may perceive the child to be subordinate in ranking, and the child may then have genuine reason to be afraid of the dog. Normality in approach by everyone concerned must be the keynote in managing your puppy correctly.

Checklist Of Considerations For Dog Ownership

1. Have we sufficient space for a dog indoors and out?
2. Can we provide companionship and interest for the dog for the greater part of each day, especially when it is young?
3. Is our garden sufficiently well fenced to keep a dog in?
4. Where will we take the dog for exercise, away from motor traffic and where it can be let off the lead easily and regularly?
5. Can we afford to feed a dog properly and pay for regular vaccinations and boosters to protect it from disease?
6. Have we budgeted for veterinary fees in illness and accident or for an insurance policy to cover those fees and our third party liability if our dog should cause an injury or damage another person's property?
7. Is our family or our environment likely to change in the foreseeable future, making the conditions for having a dog less suitable?
8. Can we make plans for the dog when we go on holiday; have we budgeted for boarding kennel expenses?
9. Do all the family really want a dog and are we willing to be responsible owners, not allowing our dog to be a nuisance in any way?
10. Are we happy to accept the inconveniences associated with dog ownership?
11. Have we the time to look after a dog, now and in the foreseeable future?

Checklist For Choice Of Dog

1. Do we want a pedigreed dog or a mongrel?
2. Do we prefer small, medium or large dogs?

3. Is that size the most suitable for our home, car and exercise ground?
4. Do we want a sporting dog, a guard, a ratter, runner or a cuddle object?
5. Do we like smooth or hairy coats, silky or rough?
6. Is anyone in the family allergic to dog hair?
7. Do we understand the grooming requirements of the dog we are considering; will we actually groom it often enough; have we somewhere to do the grooming, in summer and winter?
8. Do we want a puppy or an adult dog?
9. Do we want a dog or a bitch, or does it not matter?
10. Can we cope with a pushy, dominant dog or will a submissive one be more suitable? Or one in between?

7

DOG OR BITCH?

The next big decision is whether to have a dog or a bitch in the breeds that attract you. In some of the smaller, submissive breeds there is very little character difference between the two sexes, but in breeds where all the individuals tend to be to some degree dominant, the difference in behaviour between male and female is usually more marked. Males tend to be more self-reliant, harder characters, possibly even defiant at times in adolescence, and males may also develop embarrassing behaviour traits, but this book should be able to help you there.

The bitches are, on the whole, more affectionate and biddable. Where dogs tend to proclaim their dominance over unfamiliar canines, bitches are less inclined to do so outside the home, so in 'fighting' breeds the bitch is a better choice for exercising in public places. There are, of course, bitches with masculine tendencies and dogs that are softer characters.

Where a large breed animal is to be with women and children for most of the day a bitch is preferable and will have no less a guarding ability than the male. If there is one dog already in the household or one which is a regular visitor, it makes sense to have a new pet of the same sex. The complications of dog/bitch encounters (unless one is neutered) are too great for the average household, and it is verging on cruelty to attempt to keep a dog in the same house as an in-season bitch.

The Bitch
All bitches are subject to some degree of hormonally controlled mood swing from the time they reach puberty. This should

occur between the age of 8–12 months and thereafter heat will occur at 6–10 month intervals for the rest of her life, unless some measures are taken to avert the breeding cycle. There is no menopause in the bitch.

The average bitch will show some heightened excitability in her behaviour for a week or two before her season begins. You may also notice that the bitch does some urine marking to spread the news of her forthcoming season. Once the heat starts, her vulva begins to swell and changes go on in the vagina which will result in the blood-stained discharge which is characteristic of the start of heat. The vulval discharge of a bitch on heat lasts for about 18 days, changing from blood to straw coloured in that time. Around the tenth day of heat is the time when the bitch shows an especially intense desire for mating; this corresponds with ovulation.

The period during which the bitch accepts the male is variable, whether the red discharge has ceased or not. The urge to be mated gradually wanes, the discharge pales to white or colourless and then ceases, and the vulva returns to its normal size at between 21 and 28 days from the start of heat. At this time it is safe to allow the bitch with male dogs again.

The blood-stained discharge can be copious and will stain every surface on which the bitch sits. You will therefore want to keep her on an easily washed floor and this usually means banishment to the kitchen. This will almost certainly seem like 'punishment' to a bitch used to sharing the family fireside. Some bitches suffer considerably from this undeserved exclusion which need not happen if her cycle is suppressed by medication or she is spayed.

Bitches kept together will frequently follow each other into season and it is common for them to simulate mating play and mounting together. Unless one bitch becomes unduly irritable with another there is no need to suppress this behaviour pattern.

Because the hormonal changes in the blood of bitches are similar, whether they have been mated or not, they may display some of the signs of pregnancy, whelping and lactation six to eight weeks following the start of heat. This condition is called false pregnancy. At its greatest intensity, an unmated bitch can show a bodily enlargement which mimics pregnancy, she may make a nest, produce milk and attempt to mother inanimate objects or her own toys with all the devotion she would extend to a live litter. A strongly-affected bitch, guarding a litter which is visible only to her can be a danger when children approach her although her normal temperament may be excellent. The bitch having a false pregnancy and looking after an invisible litter is more emotionally disturbed than one which has actual puppies to guard. In some cases veterinary treatment may be needed to help the bitch over a false pregnancy.

Unfortunately it is never any use to allow the bitch to be mated and produce a litter at her next season. It will not prevent her from having a false pregnancy at the next heat, and the one after that too. In fact her false pregnancies will increase in intensity.

Spaying
The remedy recommended by most vets is to have the bitch spayed. This is a surgical operation to remove her uterus and ovaries so that she will no longer experience a hormonal cycle. In some cases the vet may advise that the cycle may be controlled by the use of hormonal preparations given orally or by injection. Bitches which are spared the breeding cycle are more consistently companionable and are less likely to suffer from diseases of the uterus or from mammary tumours.

You are strongly advised to discuss this aspect of bitch ownership when, or before, you buy a bitch puppy. If you already have an adult bitch, the best time to consult is midway between her seasons. Many bitches which come from rescue kennels have, as a matter of policy, already been spayed.

8

BUYING YOUR PUPPY

The final consideration in your selection process should be to look to the future. While the young men in the family may urge you towards a bouncy, active dog, will they be going away to work or university, leaving the dog to bounce on older people? A young married couple may enjoy taking a Setter or Pointer long-distance walking, but when children are born, it can be extraordinarily irksome to give the dog the vigorous exercise it requires when prams and pushchairs slow up progress, and the wife at home cannot leave the children to take the dog for a good walk.

If there is the possibility of having to take an elderly or infirm person to live in the household, the dog chosen must be large enough not to be tripped over and of steady temperament so that it does not make sudden movements . . . a Bulldog would be ideal.

Try to see the breeds you are considering in the homes of friends that own them. Stop owners in the street and ask about their dogs, where they got them, what they are like to live with, and the address of their vet. You are now an intending member of the dog owners' club and you will find that all the members delight in talking about their animals and can be a great deal of help to you. You can also see many breeds at dog shows, but remember the behaviour and demeanour there may be very different from the same breed at home as a companion.

The time at which you buy your puppy is also crucial to its future good management; the puppy should come into your home when you have few outside engagements, and are not expecting visitors. Christmas and other festivals are generally the most *in*appropriate times to introduce a new puppy. Your aim should be to concentrate nearly all your attention on the puppy for the first few weeks you have it . . . the more time you can devote during this period to seeing that it does the right things rather than the wrong ones, the more successful its upbringing will be.

It will entirely upset the puppy's training if it has to go into boarding kennels for more than a day or two before it is six months old, so if there is a holiday on the horizon, you will have to make plans for the puppy too.

Quarantine Regulations

Great Britain is one of the few countries in the world which is free of the dreaded fatal disease, rabies. All animal owners will want to keep it that way.

Discussions are taking place which may, ultimately, allow free movement of pet cats and dogs between countries in the European Union, including Britain. Quarantine regulations are likely to remain indefinitely between Britain and countries where rabies is endemic, including the USA. Before making any travel arrangements involving taking your dog abroad, ask for advice at your veterinary practice. Smuggling an animal in or out of Britain in contravention of regulations will result in very heavy fines, or imprisonment, and possibly the destruction of the animal.

Buying From Breeders

There are fewer large breeding kennels now, and many people feel they would rather buy from a litter reared in domestic surroundings, but that may mean waiting until the next litter is born. You should be able to have a preliminary look at the puppies when they are about four weeks old, but it is very useful to have seen the bitch before and during her pregnancy, when you have best opportunity of assessing her true temperament. Bitches may well be wary and protective when with their puppies.

Many prospective buyers feel a little embarrassed about visiting a litter in the breeder's home. They think the impersonal atmosphere of a pet shop or a puppy dealer might be easier for them. After all, we make most purchases from retail outlets where our right to make the purchase is unquestioned. But obtaining a puppy as a member of your family is very different

Fig. 7. Puppy dominance.
Or possibly precocious sexual behaviour.

from buying any other commodity. For instance, you, the buyer, will be subjected to an in-depth inquisition about your suitability to have the puppy. The ethical breeder is much more anxious than other livestock outlets about where their puppies go.

It may be that after discussion the breeder may feel obliged to say that the puppies on offer will not suit you, and although this advice may seem unacceptable at the time, please try to take it in good part. Look on the good side, the breeder knows the dogs better than you do, and you are being saved from making an expensive and possibly heart-breaking mistake.

Most breeders insist:

1.　There must be someone in your house full time.
2.　There should be a garden.
3.　There should be no children under five years old.

Young children do not handle dogs properly and if the child screams, the dog may be startled and frightened and may react badly, possibly hurting the child. To supervise a child and a puppy throughout their waking hours requires great diligence and often more time than can be spared.

Fig. 8. Test handling of puppies.
    Above: Hold the puppy up and stare into its eyes. The puppy should not resist.
    Below: Turn the puppy on to its back, the well adjusted puppy will not struggle.

This first visit to the litter should be used, on your part, to assess the general health of the litter and the surroundings in which it is being reared. If you are satisfied, you should at this stage make a tentative reservation, but you must count on making another visit when the puppies are between five and six weeks old to make your final choice. At that time, if you choose one, you should expect to deposit a substantial part of the purchase price, the balance to be paid at the time of collection. If you make a tentative reservation and then think better of it, do please let the breeder know, so that the puppy can be offered again. If you decide not to buy after a deposit has been paid, you may have to forfeit part of that deposit to pay the expenses of advertising and keeping the puppy until another buyer is found.

Pedigree Dogs
If you are buying a pedigreed dog you are entitled to expect that the litter will have been recorded at the Kennel Club so that if you should wish to show the dog, or breed later on, there will be no barrier to doing so. You may well find the puppies have all been individually registered with the breeder's Kennel Club prefix and in this case you will later be given a 'transfer form' (make sure that the breeder has signed it), so that the dog can be recorded as in your ownership at the Kennel Club.

The Pedigree
You should also receive a signed copy of the pedigree, and it is as well to understand the value of this piece of paper. At present there is no positive identification of dogs in Great Britain, so it is a matter of trust between breeder/Kennel Club and purchaser that the particulars on the pedigree form refer to the puppy you are buying. The pedigree is merely a record of the dog's ancestry going back four or five generations. Those much quoted 'pedigrees as long as your arm' are really only so much spoiled paper, because dogs beyond the fourth generation have really very little influence on the puppy in your arms. If you do not know what those dogs looked like and how they behaved, the pedigree does not tell you much.

If there are champions (usually written in red), among the parents and grandparents of your puppy, you can conclude that these dogs looked typical of their kind but you cannot tell anything about their behaviour. If the breeder has had this line of dogs for several generations, breeding from daughters and grand-daughters of the original stock, you can go some way in concluding that the line has been satisfactory in temperament, but not all the way. As we have said, keen exhibitors sometimes keep dogs for other reasons than good temperament and learning ability. While beauty shows are demanding of dogs in some ways, requiring the ability to travel very long distances and to wait for hours often in conditions of discomfort, the show dog does not need to be as versatile, adaptable and intelligent as the family pet.

Warnings Before Buying
1. **Never** buy a dog on impulse. Remember, the dog is likely to be a dependent member of your family for 12–15 years.
2. **Never** buy a dog as a surprise present; never buy a dog for anyone without consulting them first.
3. **Never** buy, or allow yourself to be given, a shy, undersized or sick dog because you are sorry for it. A dog of this kind is best left in the breeder's care.
4. **Never** buy a breed of dog without talking to other owners of the breed and, if possible, seeing the dogs in a private home. Dogs which can be managed in kennels may not be so easy in your home and your car.
5. **Never** buy a puppy, from any source, where you are not allowed to see its mother, for whatever reason!
6. **Never** buy a puppy which has travelled any distance before being offered for sale, for instance to the Home Counties from Wales or Cornwall, or to the Midlands from Scotland. Unaccompanied puppies travelling long distances are often mixed together with litters from other sources and are exposed to infection and a degree of deprivation of food and water while travelling.

    These practices should not be encouraged, so do not buy puppies that you suspect have come a long distance to the point of sale. Ask for the address of the breeder!

9

PREPARATIONS AT HOME

Before bringing your puppy home there are two important things that must be done.

1. Adequate fencing, high enough to keep your dog in when it is adult, is the primary need. Remember to protect against the dog digging under the fence to escape.

2. If you have a swimming pool or a large fish pond, be aware that puppies drown very easily if they are unable to scramble out of the water. A swimming pool partially covered in winter is a dangerous hazard even to an adult dog which may fall in, especially when there is a layer of snow on top of the cover.

Toilet Arrangements

It causes members of the public justifiable anger when footpaths, grass verges, playing fields and public places are soiled by dog faeces. In fact many places, both urban and in the country, have their own by-laws and impose significant fines on those who allow their dogs to defecate in forbidden areas or who fail to pick up and dispose of faeces their dog has passed.

Dog walkers are obliged to clean up after their own dogs and there should be pride, and not shame, in doing this. Always carry a plastic bag in your pocket as a useful means of so doing. You will be training your puppy, almost as soon as it comes to you, to use your own garden for toileting purposes. Walks should be for exercise and interest, not bowel-emptying outings.

Fig. 9. Picking up dog faeces with a plastic bag.

Faeces passed in your garden must also be picked up as soon as possible. This is the best method of preventing your puppy from acquiring the nasty habit of eating its own or other animals' faeces. (The veterinary term for this is coprophagia.) Decide how you will clear up your own garden. One of the easiest ways is to cover your gloved hand with a plastic bag, pick up the excreta, invert the bag and drop it into a plastic carrier, which can be disposed of with the household waste. More sophisticated poop-scoopers can be bought from the vet or at pet shops. An alternative method is to keep a bucket and two trowels handy, for picking up and disposing of the faeces via the household sewage system.

Never put dog faeces into your compost heap. If there are any round worm eggs in the faeces they will mature readily in decaying compost.

Puppy Territory

You have also to agree within the family in which rooms the puppy is to be allowed, whether it may sit on any furniture at all, whether it may go upstairs when it is safe to allow it to do so. It should be pointed out to those likely to transgress that it is cruel to secretly indulge a puppy by allowing it on the settee, for instance, when no-one else is looking. Treats of this kind only bring the puppy punishment later on, and also confuse its mind. Sometimes a person with an insecure outlook themselves will indulge the puppy, believing it will then care for them more, but this is not true in practice, since dogs are conditioned to give their affection and respect to the pack leader responsible for discipline.

It is quite possible to convey to the puppy within a few weeks of having it in your home that it may never set foot on carpeted areas, or may never go upstairs. Later, when the puppy is adult, indulgences may be allowed occasionally, although the dog may feel so guilty about taking advantage of the offer that it really has no pleasure from the treat. In old age, or after illness, indulgences will be more frequent and are gratefully accepted. It follows that if your puppy is forbidden the carpeted sitting room, then members of the family must expect to spend some time, especially during the evenings, in the rooms in which it is allowed, otherwise you are shutting the dog out from the pack and that may be taken as a punishment.

When you have a new puppy in the home, it is very important to perfect a 'front door drill' which all the family will follow. It is so easy for a puppy to slip out towards a road when the front door is opened to callers. The best routine is, no matter how great the urgency, to shut the puppy into the kitchen before you open a main door, and do it *always*. An alternative method would be to have the puppy's indoor kennel in the hall and to shut it in before you open the door.

Feeding the Puppy

The breeder should give you a diet sheet for the puppy. Be sure to obtain the exact foods prescribed and the same quality of milk (if given) because the puppy should be kept on exactly the same things it has been used to for at least the first two weeks in your home. Puppy foods should be kept in the refrigerator but warmed to room temperature before being fed to the puppy.

Just as much care should be taken with the puppy's food and the utensils used to prepare and serve it, as would be taken for a human baby. A puppy is just as subject to digestive upsets caused by bacteria colonising stale food or soiled dishes.

Water, in a freshly replenished small dish should be always available. Do not allow the puppy to drink water which birds may have contaminated.

Collection

Collect the puppy on a day when all the family are going to be at home but when nothing else important is happening. Mid-morning makes a good time, with the object of feeding the mid-day meal when you arrive home. Assuming that you will collect the puppy in a car, take someone who is willing to hold the puppy on their lap for this first ride. The puppy will feel more secure and is not then likely to develop phobias about car riding. Take a couple of towels for the puppy to sit on, and a cardigan to wrap around it for cosiness. If the puppy should urinate or vomit on this journey, it will not be a great disaster and no notice should be taken beyond cleaning the puppy up. The puppy should be talked to a little on the journey but not over-fussed, and there should be no visits made and no picnics which involve getting out of the car, as unvaccinated puppies should not be put down until they get back to their own garden. Get home as quickly as you reasonably can. DO NOT take the puppy to the nearest hostelry to wet its head or anything like that!

Checklist Before Bringing Puppy Home

1. Decide areas of home puppy is to use, and garden area where you will encourage excretion.
2. Check garden fence, and keep repair material available

(pups will find gaps you have overlooked). Ensure gates latch securely.

3. Reposition all trailing electricity leads and telephone cords which puppy may bite.

4. Cover sandpits (you do not want these used as lavatories) and cover and fence deep ponds and swimming pools.

5. Remove household and garden chemicals, especially the very poisonous slug pellets which are very attractive to dogs, to absolutely safe storage.

6. Make children aware of the danger of leaving plastic toys and discarded tights and stockings about. Swallowed plastic objects and articles of clothing are the cause of many surgical emergencies.

7. Arrange front door drill and make sure everyone knows about it.

8. Decide on a refuge to which the dog can retreat.

Checklist Of Supplies Required Before Bringing Puppy Home

1. Supply of food exactly in accordance with breeder's menu.

2. Gripewater (as for human babies) for hiccups and minor digestive troubles. Liquid paraffin is also very useful given by mouth or used to lubricate the rectum in cases of constipation.

3. Water bowl, food dish.

4. Hide chews (small size are best liked) and very large marrow bone.

5. Disinfectant for floors – diluted household bleach best – and carpet cleaner.

6. Mild disinfectant correctly diluted for anything which is in direct contact with puppy.

7. Bed – cardboard cartons are best for the first few months.

8. Bedding, polyester fur laid on newspaper, a soft material (to wrap around puppy if liked). Preferably not an old garment.

9. Picking-up tools and buckets for excreta.

10. Soft puppy collar and lead.

11. Vet's telephone number, and breeder's too.

12. Hot water bottle and cover.

Section III

MANAGING YOUR PUPPY

10

SOCIALISATION TIME

The modern method of managing your new puppy so that it integrates properly with your family and becomes a successful companion relies on recent discoveries about the way puppies learn and the phases of development which they go through.

The first twelve weeks of life are crucial in the puppy. For the first three weeks it will have been entirely dependent on its mother. From three weeks to twelve weeks the puppy goes through a very important socialisation period when all its attitudes to dogs, people and the outside world are being formed.

Socialisation with other dogs comes with awareness of the rest of the litter and continues until it is taken away to a new home. During this time the puppy learns how to play, how to defend itself and how to attack and generally to carry itself as a member of the canine race. It is a good thing for the puppy to have some interaction with other dogs throughout its life, but some have little opportunity for mixing once they have left the litter and yet they will still have a very good idea what being a dog is all about.

From three weeks until the time the puppy leaves the litter it is also learning to socialise with humans, first through the breeder and kennel assistants only, and later with people coming to see the litter with a view to buying. The puppy learns to recognise voices, faces and to appreciate handling, and learns to respond to actions made by humans . . . if a person bends down the puppy will come to them . . . the puppy will stand on its hind legs in the play pen, 'asking' to be picked up, etc. Between seven and fourteen weeks is the critical period for socialisation with humans. It is crucial to recognise and fully use this period of special susceptibility in order to fashion your puppy into an adaptable and well-rounded dog personality.

Mishandling during these socialisation periods can create problems that are difficult, perhaps even impossible, to erase later. An added difficulty is that the effect of this mishandling may not be noticeable at first, but may be triggered later by some trauma or specific situation in adult life.

The particular problems that can arise are aggression and shyness or nervous habits. Puppies are especially impression-able between eight and twelve weeks of age, and an experi-ence that produces acute fear at this time may 'mark' a puppy for life, especially one which has already some hereditary tendency to nervousness or shyness. It is for this reason that managing the puppy during its first weeks in your home, so that it does the right things and has little opportunity to do wrong, is so important to its future life. Hard punishment should be avoided at this time, and in this sense punishment includes leaving the puppy on its own to be lonely and frightened. The chart on page 76 will show that the puppy is not at this time capable of any calculated act which deserves punishment, beyond the word NO!

If you have obtained your puppy from a reputable breeder the canine socialisation will have taken place and the human socialisation will have been begun with tact and care, giving you good material with which to continue. The kennelised puppy which has not been handled or had 'house' experience has bigger shocks to come when you take it into your home, so you have a harder task to face. It is important that you do not delay obtaining your puppy beyond the eight-week age, especially where bigger breeds are concerned, such as the German Shep-herd Dogs, Rottweilers, Dobermans and Boxers, which can tend to be dominant.

As the 8–12 week stage is one in which the puppy should not have any fear-provoking experiences, it is important that the puppy should not be left alone for more than three hours, except overnight, and it would be preferable if it was not left for as long as that. The natural instinct of an isolated animal, especially one which has so lately come from a 'pack' is to try to escape by digging, and chewing, and drawing attention to its plight by crying and howling.

This is a natural protective move which serves a useful purpose in the wild and is not, at this stage, punishable behaviour, but if the puppy has occasion to use this escape behaviour often, because you leave it unreasonably long, then the behaviour pattern becomes imprinted and you will have a dog which can never be left without its destroying its surroundings.

The puppy so far has had all its needs supplied by its mother, its first pack leader. Later, the breeder assumes the pack leader role, supplying food, comfort and keeping away danger in whatever form it appears . . . such as breaking up too aggressive play. In order to give your puppy an atmosphere of security in which to adjust to life and grow into a confident well-balanced dog, you, the owner, must now assume the pack leader and provider role. Being a pack leader does not imply that you only dole out discipline; you protect and comfort too, and you order the puppy's life so that it is all enjoyable. Doing what the pack leader wants is a natural response, although there will be, as the puppy grows up, some degree of rebellion unless it is a very submissive character.

When your puppy accepts you as its protector and pack leader, you should see that, during the critical period for socialisation at 8 to 12 weeks, the puppy encounters as many types of people as possible, including women, men and children. The puppy should also at this time be 'exposed' within your protection to a variety of experiences. Unfortunately, the puppy will not be able to walk out on the lead as the inoculation programme will not be completed until 12 or 14 weeks old, but you can carry your puppy down the High Street and let it hear traffic noise, whistles and hoots from within the safety of your arms, and a very important event in its young life will be the visit to the veterinary surgeon for its vaccinations.

The puppy may, quite understandably, be frightened when confronted with noise or large vehicles, and although you will be offering comfort, it should be in the nature of 'jollying along' and not tender sympathy, because that reinforces the idea that there is something to fear. The veterinary surgeon will be skilled in handling animals and giving injections and he and his staff

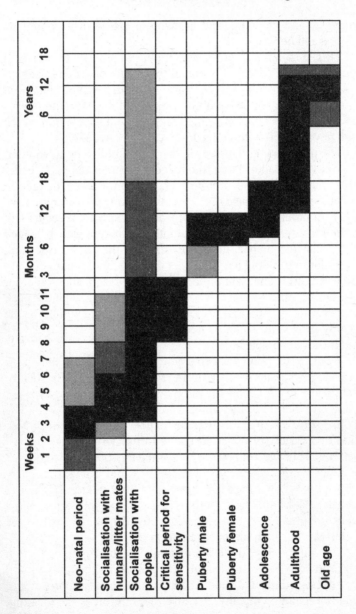

Fig. 10. Social development of the dog.
Most critical periods shown in the blackest tone.

will all combine with you to make the visit to the vet's a pleasurable experience, thus laying down a good foundation for visits in the future. If the puppy should yelp at the entry of the hypodermic needle, the momentary pain is very soon forgotten, especially if you, the pack leader, are being bright and breezy and showing no apprehension or fear emotion at all. If you are upset or tremulous yourself, then the puppy will conclude that this is a place where fear is justified. You may, if you wish, have a tiny food reward ready to give as the vaccination is done, but this could become a habit which will be unwelcome if the dog has to have an anaesthetic, so it is better avoided. Just make the visit 'one of the nice things we do'.

Reward Good Behaviour – Ignore Bad
If the puppy tends to be shy, ignore that and jolly it along towards being bold, never sympathise and pet it unless something accidental and unjust has happened, like being stepped on ... then fuss and apology are warranted, but otherwise, assume that life is good and take care that, from the puppy's point of view, it *is* good. This involves you as pack leader in providing warmth, food, shelter and companionship and a security from which to sum up all the new experiences life is releasing on to the puppy.

Submitting to grooming, nail clipping and ear cleaning is another thing which has to become part of the puppy's routine ... give a short time to this each day and stop only when the puppy is submitting quietly; it is a mistake to give up when the puppy is struggling ... it may conclude that it has *won*. Try not to let struggling occur. Praise, laugh and be happy afterwards, your tone of voice in all dealings with the puppy is very important. In these weeks you may find that you are frequently obliged to praise, laugh and be happy; will that be doing you good too? You may find in the puppy a significant lift to your own spirits, and it will be rewarding to see how well the puppy responds to the teaching you provide.

In these early weeks when the puppy is being socialised no deterrents should be used, indeed, the puppy is not capable of knowing about right and wrong yet. You will, of course, sometimes have to deter the puppy from some danger, and then the word NO is the most important in your vocabulary. Say it very sharply, and rather loudly and make sure it is obeyed by ceasing the action the puppy was making. At this stage, follow the NO with a diversion of some kind to interest the puppy in something else, just as you would a very young child. Unfortunately, we cannot reason with puppies and say, 'Don't touch that, it is sharp or hot . . .' We can only get into the dog's mind that there are some objects, some areas, utterly forbidden to it.

11

THE WAY A DOG LEARNS

Ivan Petrovich Pavlov, the Russian physiologist working at the end of the 19th century, found out that dogs could learn by classical conditioning. The ringing of a bell at any time brought the conditioned response of salivation and readiness for a meal. This is not the main way the dog in our home learns to behave. Far more important to us is what scientists call 'instrumental conditioning'. This means, in simple terms, 'the action brings its own reward'.

Dogs learn as a result of doing things, and the keynote of our system of dog management is to let the dog learn from doing the right things. We try to give the dog no opportunity to do wrong.

We have a certain amount of difficulty in communicating with dogs because they have no language and they cannot link a current action with something they did some time ago. A dog which is learning a behaviour pattern can only establish the rightness of its action if it is rewarded by approval or a tangible reward within two or three seconds of the action being performed. This is why correction of misdeeds is so difficult.

In colloquial terms the dog cannot understand 'what you are on about' if the misdeed happened ten or twenty minutes ago. You may say that your dog has a sense of guilt – 'he knows when he has done wrong' – but this is a reaction to your tone of voice and your facial expression. If you always come home to rage at the mess in the kitchen, your dog's permanent reaction to your return home may be one of guilt. He does not know what it is that sets you off but he knows that you certainly come home in a nasty mood! Likewise, when you are training a puppy, if you give the praise too late after a good action the dog enjoys your benevolence but does not know what he has done to deserve it.

The 'reward' learning method works in this way: you want your dog to lie down, so every time he does so, you immediately say the word 'Down', praise him or give a delicious food reward. After a very short time the dog will make the association and will lie down in anticipation of being praised or getting something to eat . . . just as Berry, the Boxer, rolls on her back to trigger this reaction in her owner.

Because the dog soon finds that its action has a positive reinforcement, that is, it 'pays off' according to the dog's outlook, the dog will tend to repeat the action, and it has learnt to do one thing which you want.

Give the dog a verbal cue by saying 'Sit', showing once or twice the position you mean by that hissing S-i-i-i-t sound, and when the dog drops into that position, you reward it immediately. The dog will soon make the association between the hissing sound and the need to fold up its back legs so that it receives the reward in a body position which pleases its pack leader. It has been found that to be most effective the reward must be given within half a second of the dog making the right response. Berry was taught to sit in ten minutes after dinner one night by calling her and giving her one broad bean every time she dropped into the sit position. Alas, she vomited all over the carpet afterwards, broad beans not being the most suitable puppy food but the thing most handy at the time. She has never forgotten what sit means, in fact she seems to feel that 'sit' should bring her a round of applause every time!

Of course, the value of the reward and the motivation the dog feels to do the action varies . . . a tired, sleepy puppy, with a tummy full after a good meal may be very slow to respond to 'Sit' even with the certainty of a reward.

If the reward stops coming . . . that is, if Berry continually rolls on to her back soliciting play and praise, but her owner is too preoccupied with work to notice her, then she will assume this attitude less often, and eventually give it up altogether . . . it has ceased to 'pay off' as far as she is concerned. This is called 'extinction' of a behaviour pattern.

If Berry is noticed when she does her rolling trick, quite often, but not always, this supplies her with an incentive to try harder, to do it more often to see if she is going to be lucky this time, and so, once a dog has learned a piece of behaviour (or a trick), rewards should be given only from time to time at varying intervals. The same principle applies when people play fruit machines, there just might be a reward coming at the next pull of the handle.

These two methods – regular reward and then intermittent reward – are the secret behind much of the training of police and army dogs which perform such useful service, sometimes perfecting far more intricate tasks than is generally known. The same ploys may be used to train dogs out of bad habits they have acquired.

Discipline does have its place (but not with puppies under three months old). An appropriate corrective action can be effective in older puppies and adults, but, like the reward, the correction must occur immediately the offence has been committed, and correction must be applied consistently and fairly. Loosing one's temper, punishing too hard or too late and for something the dog cannot understand, does nothing to get you a more obedient dog. It may get you a cringing one, or it may get you a resentful one, but not a good dog.

The result of applying harsh punishment is the possibility of creating anxiety and aggressive feelings in the dog. Any deterrent must be of sufficient strength the first time it is used to disrupt the unwanted behaviour but not so strong as to frighten the dog and to shake its faith in its pack leader.

Quite often you will find, after you have lost your temper over something the dog has done, that really the culprit was yourself . . . you left your best shoes where he could get them, you left the cupboard door open so that he could get all the contents out. Be fair to the dog, but it is no use apologising now; he will not know what you are contrite about.

If you find the dog has committed some error some time ago, just ignore it, clear up or put things to rights, not commenting to the dog at all, either cheerfully or crossly.

A canine pack leader will punish another dog by jumping on its back and rubbing the offender's nose in the mud. Honour then being satisfied, both parties get up and walk away and soon after will be found curled up in the same bed together. We cannot hope to discipline our dogs in the same way; we cannot expect to be quick enough or accurate enough; we might get hurt or the whole episode might turn into a game and therefore become a reward for the dog.

Magic

Both authors of this book have found that magic discipline is by far the most effective. The thrown object which strikes a dog while it is actually committing a crime acts as a great deterrent while not really hurting the dog at all. The secret is that the action takes place when no human being is anywhere near . . . there is an all-seeing eye which knows when a dog is up to mischief!

When Anna the Doberman was young, she enjoyed making raids on the handbag of the lady of the house. In order to stop this happening we set up a trap. We deliberately left the bag in a suitable place, and, having armed ourselves with a small bean-bag, waited until Anna put her nose into the handbag and then wham! Something sped through the air and landed on Anna's rear, startling her and inflicting retribution although no humans were near, and no-one shouted.

Dogs watch their humans so much that they can predict many of our actions. The most agile of us are so much clumsier than dogs so they can easily predict what we are about to do. But the invisibly thrown object is unpredictable and anything which takes a dog by surprise makes a very strong impression. Hand-bags were quite safe from Anna after that; this same remedy could be adapted to other situations too. We once had a kennels situated in an old orchard. Little apples broke up many unwanted behaviour patterns among our Boxers.

The thrown object also serves as a distraction, even if it misses the dog. By the time he has investigated the beanbag or whatever has been thrown, the sequence of behaviour has been broken up and may not be started again.

A child's water pistol is another magic weapon which can be used to disturb a dog committing a crime . . . this is very effec-tive used from an upstairs window. None of these deterrents *hurt* and they are not degrading to the owner, as physical violence can be. If the magic is cleverly done the dog will not associate the owner with the action at all.

An unexpected reaction by objects which the dog is actually in the act of attacking works very well too . . . the dog so nimble with its paws that it can open cupboards will never trust that cupboard again if a carefully devised 'booby trap' of a pile of tins falls out next time. These 'magic' deterrents are much more effective even than hitting the dog as it opens the cupboard, if you should be lucky enough to see the deed being done. It is probably the surprise element when the dog feels itself to be unobserved, and the lack of any preliminary movement or warning which does the trick. If the booby trap could somehow be wired to a sound recording of the owner's voice, that would probably represent the ultimate in the unexpected.

Fig. 11. The booby trap in action.

Ignoring the dog and the withdrawal of attention and petting can also be a punishment, effective in the long term when a dog is dominating or bullying one member of the family. The ploy should be for all the rest of the humans to turn off the dog completely, never letting even the eyes rest upon it, while the dominated or bullied person provides all food, walks, and other forms of comfort or indulgence. The dog then *has* to turn to that person. This regime works well, provided all the family co-operate and never forget that they are not supposed to be relating to the dog at all over this rehabilitation period.

Putting the dog into solitary confinement can be counterproductive to your purpose and it is quite inadvisable in young puppies during the socialisation period. The problem is that the dog may not make the association between 'solitary' and crime and the next time you leave the dog when you are going out, it may assume that the last thing it did before you shut the door upon it was a 'crime' . . . a pity if this was going into the garden to be clean!

These principles of learning are the ones you will put into use from the time when you first get your puppy. Later on you may feel that the puppy needs some reminding of the things it must not do, and even later, the deterrent may be needed to show that some behaviour patterns are just not permitted in this family. But too strong a discipline is unfair to a family pet. Teach very firmly the commands which keep your puppy away from danger, teach immaculate housetraining as soon as the puppy has complete elimination control, put things away so that damage is minimised and otherwise, just enjoy living together!

The Secrets of Dog Training
1. Reward the dog very quickly for a correct response.
2. Give verbal praise but intermittently give a small food reward which the dog will value.
3. The dog learns most quickly if the reward is forthcoming every time it responds correctly.
4. The dog retains the behaviour pattern you have taught for longer, so that it becomes a habit, if the rewards are given only sometimes.
5. If the dog is not rewarded at all, it may lose the behaviour

pattern unless it suits the dog to retain it.

6. Corrective measures for inappropriate behaviour must be given very quickly, whether it is a sharp NO or more stern action.

7. Corrective measures should startle the dog but not make it afraid. Magic, especially in set-up situations, will quickly teach dogs what is not acceptable.

8. Ideally dogs should be allowed to 'escape' into a behaviour which is acceptable to avoid stern corrective measures.

12

HOUSETRAINING

The chart opposite shows the comparison between the puppy and the human infant and may help you to be tolerant of the puppy's failings while it is young, especially when you consider how much more patient we have to be with human babies.

Gestation time in the bitch is short, and her puppies have to be equipped to fend for themselves very early in life. Born with ears and eyes undeveloped, within a month of birth the puppy can see, hear and stand. At eight weeks it can run and play constructively with its littermates, it will move away from the nest to urinate and defecate, and it will never urinate during sleep. The puppy can run towards a person who attracts its attention, and it is beginning to learn to associate sounds with action you require it to take. The brain capacity is developing towards acquiring knowledge about the world in which it is to live. At the age of eight weeks the puppy can achieve far more in every way than a human baby.

The puppy can control bladder and bowel movement for a few minutes at eight weeks old but it cannot convey the necessity to humans, unless they are watching the instinctive and quite identifiable movements the puppy makes before the act. Fairly reliable control is reached in the puppy from the age of four months, and 95 per cent of puppies will be entirely reliable by the age of eight mouths, a state which we do not expect in the human infant until three or four years, perhaps as old as six years. Elimination control will relax during illness, such as an episode of loose bowel movements, extreme agitation, or, of course, being unable to get outside to be clean, but

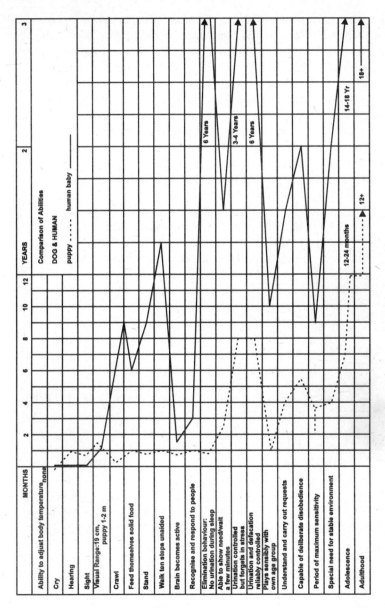

Fig. 12. Comparison of abilities chart.

this restriction will also apply to a child up to six years or even beyond. We have in the puppy considerably less nuisance over toilet training than we do in our own young, so it seems unreasonable to lose patience with a puppy for 'dirtiness' when our own species are completely uncontrolled, and in a far more labour-intensive way, for at least five times as long!

There have been cases of newly acquired puppies being rejected within a few days because they are 'messing all over the house'. This excuse, for that is what it is, reflects badly only on those that make it. The puppy should not be 'all over the house'. It should be restricted to those areas where there are people to watch it, preferably on uncarpeted floors, and the puppy's elimination needs should be anticipated. In puppies, as in babies, feeding and elimination follow each other very quickly, so you must be ready to take the puppy outside the *instant* it has finished eating. As puppies do not urinate during sleep after 2½ weeks old, you will also need to be ready when the puppy wakes. Agitation and being left alone, or crying, will certainly make the puppy pass urine.

You will notice that during play, the puppy will sniff around the floor in a tight circle, probably assuming a worried expression, when it has the urge to eliminate, but the interval between *indication* and *doing* is very short. If you are busy or preoccupied the puppy may soil the floor and it can be very difficult to be alert all the time when you are cooking or talking on the telephone. The time between indication and elimination gets longer with age, as it does with a child, and the puppy at 4–5 months will give you a much clearer signal, progressing to actual 'asking' in some very plain fashion to go out. They usually stare at the door, or bang at it with their paws. Berry, the Boxer, will press down on the door handle and let herself out, the height of sophisticated training. This was a trick she discovered for herself, which has been subsequently reinforced by reward.

Adult dogs and bitches normally last for several hours without urinating (unless they are territory marking). In summer when doors are standing open, you have no occasion to think of the dog's needs, except perhaps first thing in the morning and late at night. In winter, the fully house-trained dog can be asked to go into the garden 'to be good' and it will then eliminate on command, provided you reward it as noted before when it performs.

The word or phrase you use for housetraining must be decided when you get the puppy and it must then be used every time the act is performed in the right place. It is quite hard to find a word that is acceptable to use in public and one which will not be used in any other context. Generations of Boxers have responded to 'go and be good' although they know that 'she is so *good*' is a universal form of praise, which, when used indoors, does not cause the fountain to flow. It is the sound and inflection which dogs recognise and not the actual words. 'Outside', or 'go and be clean' are other acceptable phrases for housetraining. Anna, the Doberman, will urinate at the sound of an undulating whistle, a refined signal indeed.

With your newly acquired puppy, you will have to go out into the garden, and *stay with the puppy*, repeating your chosen phrase over and over until the puppy performs, when you will congratulate it most enthusiastically. By the association technique, the puppy will eventually connect the doing with the phrase, and later, you can fling the door wide and use the phrase, and the dog will go out to eliminate without delay. While you may, to a large extent, leave your adult to take care of its own needs, it is extremely useful to keep the phrase within the dog's memory, so that if you are away from home, or on a car journey, you can ask your dog to do the necessary and get results very quickly even on strange ground.

We have said that the puppy will indicate that it is going to pass urine and that you have a very short time in which to get it outside. Puppies have very little power of concentration, like toddlers, and once in the garden, the puppy may look at the flowers or chase a butterfly, quite forgetting what the mission was all about. Staying with the puppy takes patience on your part, but there is no way to avoid this part of the management. Keep an umbrella handy by the door, but take as comfort that thousands and thousands of other new puppy owners are also walking the garden in their pyjamas in the dawn hours. Turning the young puppy out on its own is quite useless; as the door shuts upon it, the puppy's whole attention turns to getting back inside with the rest of the household pack.

If the puppy is very young or fragile and the weather outside is very bad it may be advisable to keep the puppy indoors for a week or two and to allow it to eliminate on pads of newspaper placed near the door you will eventually use to take it to the garden for toilet purposes. Do not cover the whole floor with papers, just the immediate vicinity of the door so that the puppy associates going to this area when it has the need to pass urine or faeces. Try to use fresh newspaper, not paper which has been stored where it may have been contaminated by rats or mice. The puppy will be used to the newspaper surface because breeders cover their puppy pens with paper.

When the puppy is able to go outside to urinate and pass faeces, it helps to move a piece of already soiled paper out into the garden so that the puppy associates the place it has previously used with what you are asking it to do now.

Remember, when you are housetraining a puppy it is essential to go out with the puppy and to stay with it, repeating your special code-word for the action required and being ready to show great pleasure when the puppy does the right thing. The puppy will learn nothing at all if you just push it outside on its own; it will wait for the door to be opened and then deposit its waste matter on your carpet. You must teach, teach, teach all the time.

Your nights will be shorter when you are housetraining a puppy as dogs are usually awakened by sounds of activity outside at first light. Take the puppy out immediately it wakes you and also very last thing at night.

13

THE FIRST DAY & NIGHT IN YOUR HOME

Your loving, caring relationship with the puppy begins the moment the breeder hands over the puppy to you. Your aim from then on is to make this little creature a happy subordinate in your family pack – not a persecuted or cowed one. Each person must work at making a good relationship with the dog. Consistency as individuals and as a family is the keynote.

Managing Children
Young children are sometimes delighted to have a pack member below them in the family. They will try to order the puppy about unnecessarily and may try to administer punishment, possibly the same kind of slaps they receive themselves. They may also call the puppy at inappropriate times and in many ways produce a confusion in the puppy's mind which will hamper your proper management. A definite demarcation line should be established between those family members who may manage and train the puppy and those who may not.

Close observation should always be kept on games involving a puppy or a young dog with children, lest either side becomes over-excited or inappropriately treated. It can be wise to remove a puppy or dog from the scene when other children come in to play. The dog may interpret rowdy play as a threat to its young 'pack members' or to their toys and may show hostility to the visitors with dire consequences.

Human Health Precautions
There are a few general rules about new puppies which it is

advisable to observe, in order that there shall not be the slightest health risk to humans or dog.

1. Never let the dog eat from plates used by the family; always feed it in its own bowl.
2. Pick up and dispose of the dog's excreta as soon as possible after it has been passed.
3. All the family should wash their hands after handling the puppy and before eating or preparing food.
4. Because of the small, but significant risk of infection by puppy roundworm (toxocara canis), be extra careful that children's faces and hands are washed frequently and always before sleep, or eating. Puppy roundworm is not the same as, or the cause of, the very prevalent *threadworms* in children.
5. Try to discourage the puppy from licking children.

The First Few Hours
Your puppy, having travelled happily in your arms from the breeder's premises, will be ready to urinate immediately you reach your home, so carry it straight to the part of the garden you mean to use, put it down, and say your urination phrase over and over again. Many people think it would be best if the puppy used the bottom of the garden, well out of the way, but remember, you will be going as well, in bad weather, late at night and early, and you have no time to change into outdoor shoes, so you may decide it would be prudent to use a patch near the house.

You should, this first time, have an easy success, because the need will be already there, so when the puppy has performed, praise it and pet it as if it had just won a gold medal, and then bring it indoors. This would be a good time to offer a small drink, and then to let the puppy spend half an hour exploring the kitchen without too much human interference. This will be a big landmark in the puppy's development; it may be the first time it has been outside of a playpen, it will be the first time it has been without its litter mates, and there will be a whole lot of huge skyscraper objects to be looked at, smelt and assessed.

You may find the puppy tends to get behind or under furniture. This may not be through fear, but because the strength of the general lighting is too strong. Young puppies avoid strong daylight for some weeks after they can see quite well in subdued light.

Puppies may also be nervous of wind and blowing trees at first, and also of the sound of your household appliances which may have a different note from the ones used by the breeder. Children must be taught that it is cruel to make loud sounds, or hissing sounds, right into the puppy's ear, or to startle the puppy in any way. As the dog grows older, mistreatment of this kind may precipitate an attack on the child which, while regrettable, will not be strictly the dog's fault. Because the dog's reaction to mistreatment is so instinctive and instant, it should be easy for a child to understand that teasing in any form is forbidden.

Unfortunately, many adults know no other form of play than teasing and this is a pity, particularly with a sensitive puppy. In the early days, the puppy must have a fair chance in any game that is played, and it should be allowed to win little contests, but never big ones. You must decide when playtime is over. The puppy must always allow handling, and always give up a 'prize' to an adult human. It is not wise to allow little children to take things from a possessive dog.

After the puppy has explored for a while it should be fed, in accordance with the breeder's instructions. Take it outside again immediately to be clean and follow the procedure as before. The puppy should be ready for a sleep in the warmly-lined carton or wire crate you have prepared for it in a cosy corner in the kitchen . . . check for draughts at the floor level.

Your puppy has made a very big transition from the warmth and security of its litter and its mother to a very different life in your home. It is useful now to continue your bonding by staying in the room where the puppy is sleeping, keeping busy on tasks, of course, but staying within sight in case the puppy should stir in its sleep. You can, with advantage, sing and chat to the puppy, and have the radio on; absolute quiet is not a necessity but it is not wise to disturb the puppy while it is asleep, as, like all babies, it does need secure sleep to enable it to grow in mind and body. Be ready to pick up the puppy and take it outside to be clean immediately it wakes up . . . and so the routine goes on through the day. We did say you needed plenty of free time! But in a short while you will have won, provided you manage to avoid accidents occurring.

Naming The Puppy

This is an immediate necessity, for you will want to use the name at every possible opportunity to get it embedded in the puppy's mind. A short crisp name which all the family can pronounce in the same way is ideal. Rover, the favourite dog name in Edwardian times, has gone completely out of use now that it is anti-social and dangerous for dogs to wander outside their owner's premises. Pick up the puppy, look straight into its face and say, 'You are Pixie', or whatever name has been chosen. Use the name when the puppy is coming towards you, when you put its food down, and when you are playing, so that the puppy has every chance to get to know its 'signal'. In the first few hours in your home the puppy has begun learning to use the garden for toilet purposes, and begun learning its name, two very big steps towards maturity.

The First Night

The day which for all the family has been so exciting will eventually wind down to bedtime. Because it is so important to reinforce the pack leader's role of protector and comforter before you become a disciplinarian also, and because most of us regard cleanliness within the house of prime importance, if you are so inclined take the puppy and its box into your bedroom and put it beside the bed, so that you can be within touch of the puppy all night.

The traditional way is to leave the puppy downstairs safely tucked up in its cardboard box with a well covered warm hot water bottle and possibly a clock to resemble its mother's heartbeat. You may have to endure some crying and you will probably feel you must go down two or three times during the night to quieten the puppy. Eventually, after a week or two of this performance, the puppy will accept being alone for most of the night, but has this been good for your intention of bonding with the puppy? The answer has to be no. What has your little pup done to deserve to be shut away alone, probably frightened and possibly cold, after the day that was so enjoyable?

To continue the bonding and to reinforce the housetraining which you have already started, the puppy should stay close beside you, either with a member of the family in their bedroom, or one family member can sleep with the puppy in its bedroom, presumably the kitchen or utility room. This regime may have to last for about two weeks, until the puppy is really familiar with its sleeping quarters, the new regime and with you. Consider establishing the security which you would give to a young child and you will not go far wrong. Then there will be no set-back to your relationship because the puppy has not experienced any distress or fear during this very sensitive period of adjustment.

The wire crate or indoor kennel which has been mentioned several times before will come into its most important role when the puppy is taken into a bedroom to sleep. With the door shut, and the roof piece open so that you can reach in to touch the puppy, you have the ideal way of looking after your pet overnight and the opportunity to rush it outside first thing in the morning. And the crate can easily be folded and brought downstairs to be used where it is wanted all day.

Eventually, when the puppy is fully familiar with you and your home you may wish to change the sleeping arrangements, or you may feel that your dog's place is beside you always, as your companion and your security. Follow your own inclinations and do not feel that you have to conform to anyone else's ideas in this very personal matter.

14

THE NEXT FEW WEEKS

The puppy's first full day in your home begins with going outside again, being praised for action, being called by its name when it is approaching already, and by the word NO when it is advancing on anything which is to be forbidden.

The four or five meals advised by the breeder should be served at regular times and have water always available, even if the puppy is having milky meals. The puppy should be wakened for meals but not for any other purpose, as it requires a lot of sleep. Take the opportunity to stand the puppy on a covered table for a few seconds, gradually increasing the time, to prepare for the day when the veterinary surgeon will want to examine it, and begin the grooming routine, even if the puppy has very little coat to comb at this age. If the puppy has the type of coat to be bathed often, start the use of a hair-dryer early in life.

The puppy will be going on with its exploring and having new experiences, and being handled by new people as friends come to see your lovely puppy. As the puppy gets to regard its box as its home, it will be useful to leave it for a short while, even ten minutes, while you go into another room, so that the puppy begins to have the experience of being alone; your return should be cheerful, not too sympathetic even if the puppy is crying, but at this stage, you should not allow the puppy to cry for very long. Never give the puppy the impression that it has only to squeak to bring you running, puppies will quickly learn to exploit that. Praise the puppy if it has been good, ignore other behaviour at this stage.

Keep always in your mind the maxim that the puppy is not to be distressed or unhappy.

Playthings
There are many toys which you can buy for puppies. It is up to
you to make sure they are suitable and not in any way dangerous. Toys with a squeaker in are really very unsuitable, as the
sound of the high-pitched squeak can make some dogs frantic,
and then their object becomes to 'kill' the toy and get the squeak
out. If this is swallowed, an expensive operation to remove an
intestinal blockage could result, so these cheap toys are worth
nothing at all.

Nylabone make some excellent white nylon bone and ring
shapes which withstand a lot of chewing without disintegrating.
Some of the best toys currently available are made by Pedigree
Petfoods and sold in veterinary surgeries. These are exceedingly
durable rubber toys in simple shapes which seem to have a
random bounce built in, to make throwing and catching more
fun.

A length of thick rope from a ship's chandler can be a
favourite toy, great for tugging games or towing around. Be
very careful about the size of the ball you give your dog. A dog
will catch a small ball which can lodge in the back of the throat
so that the dog will choke unless the obstruction is very
promptly removed. Saliva rapidly covering the ball makes
extraction very difficult. The way to remove the ball is to put
both hands either side of the dog's head behind the ears and
press forwards, hoping to propel the ball out. You may also use
the handle of a spoon behind the object to bring it within reach.
The dog may easily die if help is not provided quickly.

Rawhide chews are very popular, and less messy than bones,
and a quoit ring gives a lot of fun. Some things, such as a strong
polythene bucket, amuse the puppy very well and are safe to
play with provided they are removed when it becomes possible
to swallow pieces of the material.

It is usual to say that it is unwise to give old shoes and
gloves, or pieces of cotton cloth to pull, as the puppy cannot
distinguish between these discarded things and good ones.
This is a valid theory, but when there is so much mileage to be
got from an old leather shoe in terms of dogplay, and we need
to give them a variety of interests and activities, it seems a
pity to consign a good play object straight to the dustbin. We

may also be crediting the dog with too much discernment, if we allow a hide chew, but not a hide glove or shoe . . . the shape and colour look very different to us, but we really do not know how they look to a puppy.

With Anna, we did not feel confident enough to take the chance of giving clothing or shoes as our boys were always liable to leave good garments lying around, even in the garden. We elected to give her three things only: a football, a cricket ball and a hardwood log. She has never chewed on anything else or chewed any item of clothing, although the log is now down to an almost round ball of wood through prolonged chewing on it.

You can teach a dog what is permitted by giving used clothing as toys only in certain locations. A shoe given to the dog and kept in the garden or the kitchen is a toy; shoes and gloves in the bedroom must not be touched. And if a new pair of shoes should be left in the kitchen? Sorry, but that is your fault! Berry has been one of the hardest and most destructive dogs encountered in a whole lifetime of dog keeping, but although she sleeps in our bedroom and is now of an age when she can get out of her box and walk around during the night if she wishes, she has never touched any article of clothing in the bedroom, although old shoes, and pieces of cotton cloth are part of her toy collection.

It is not a bad thing to live by the maxim NO DOG OR PUPPY EVER COMMITS ANY CRIME. The bad episodes happen because people ALLOWED THEM TO HAPPEN, either by sins of omission (not supervising the dog, or leaving it alone unreasonably long) or by sins of commission (leaving precious articles where the dog can get at them). Not shutting doors to sitting rooms and bedrooms can be a major crime in a puppy-owning home, and being untidy is just as bad. Perfection in humans and dogs is impossible to obtain, and there will be some teeth marked objects during puppy days, but it is really up to the family to see that damage is minimal. You cannot be promised that all the joy a dog will bring your family will not be balanced in a small way by some losses, but with care and forethought the damage should be minimal.

Since it is very difficult to keep an eye on the puppy at all times through the day, there are bound to be some puddles on the floor, but if the puppy is kept on a newspaper covered surface, the cleaning should be quite easy. Do wash up all mistakes, preferably with diluted bleach, as a pine disinfectant seems to accentuate the smell of urine, and puppies will return to the same spot again and again. Every act of elimination done outside on command is a step towards housetraining, every one inside the house is a step back and it is really up to the owner to determine which way progress shall go.

If you must leave the puppy for an hour or so, you must expect that it will have needed to pass urine or faeces, and there must be NO PUNISHMENT . . . what alternative would a young creature, human or animal have? As the puppy grows up, you may express a little disapproval as you clean up, to show that you are not overjoyed to have to do this, but if the puppy could not get out, if there was no-one to ask, then there can be no blame. Pulling the puppy over to the mess, or the really primitive 'rubbing his nose in it', gives you a puppy with a dirty, smelly face, and nothing more. Remember, toddlers make similar messes for very much longer, even when people are with them constantly, so have patience with your puppy. Dogs are very quickly and easily housetrained if they have the opportunity to make their needs known.

Collars

During the first week it is a good idea to let the puppy wear a soft collar for a few minutes each day . . . it will scratch at the collar, but in the end it will become a habit to wear it. Anna now feels incomplete without her collar and shows anxiety when it is removed. Later, attach a leash and let it trail behind the puppy. As you pass, pick it up occasionally, and let the puppy walk a few steps 'on the lead' before letting go again, so that it has some idea of feeling control by the lead before more formal training begins.

Handling

While your puppy is tiny, you should pick it up frequently, and let other responsible adults do so as well. The puppy is not allowed to struggle, it should not be put down until it is quiet in the holder's arms, and it is a good idea to ask responsible people to put a comb through the coat, turn back the ears, and to go through other movements so that the puppy is not orientated to handling in this way by only one person.

Car Rides
During the first week it is a good idea to take the puppy for short trips in the car, even a deliberate ride to the end of the road and back, to reinforce car travel in its mind. Hold the puppy in the arms at first, later on it should go on the back seat, or for a small breed, in a wire crate. Dog guards, confining the dog to the back end of estate cars are very fashionable, and are particularly necessary if there are several children to occupy the seats, but if there is a shunting-type crash, the dog takes the impact first. Crates are also being used in cars increasingly often, even for big dogs, but the dog is then restricted in room and also ventilation, and it cannot move to the shady side of the car in hot weather. It is better to have your dog trained to behave well than to buy expensive apparatus to keep it in.

Most puppies drool and are sick when they are first taken out in the car, so it makes sense to take some experimental short rides while the puppy gets used to the idea. Plan to take the puppy out before its next meal, not after!

Always Praise & Reward
Do not forget the praise when the dog has done well, with or without the food reward. It is all too easy to say nothing when the dog fulfils your wish, but to remonstrate volubly when it does not, and we all know what a word of praise does for our own egos.

When giving food rewards, have a care to the total dietary intake; you could be giving the dog something close to double rations if you reward it often. A crumb of sweet biscuit, the smallest scrap of cheese rewards a puppy; beware of using vitaminised preparations too heavily; it is harmful to give more than the manufacturer's recommendations.

When the puppy is completely at home in your house, but not on the day it is being wormed or has had vaccinations, you can, if you intend to, start the puppy sleeping in the kitchen. Make sure the little dog is tired when it goes to bed. It will, by now, be familiar with the room and the bed, and if you make it cosy with a hot water bottle, it should go down without fuss, and remain quiet until early morning, when you will have to try to hear the lark first, in order to save the puppy making a puddle and going back on the early housetraining. Some dogs are of much more independent natures than others; some will not mind being alone, others will feel it keenly, and in such case, if the puppy is no trouble while it is with you, you may decide to leave the sleeping arrangements as they began. Later in its life, it makes sense to have a dog which can protect the vulnerable parts of the house rather than one shut in the kitchen, not usually very rewarding territory for burglars.

There are increasing numbers of cases being reported of dogs being poisoned by fumes from solid fuel boilers when shut in kitchens and utility rooms overnight. Make sure the puppy's sleeping place is ventilated and the boiler regularly serviced.

Basic Training
When your puppy is firmly established in your home and is confident and happy, then is the time to begin on the basic obedience training which will make your dog acceptable anywhere. The usual basic commands are Sit, Down, Stay and Come, but any words that you choose are acceptable. There should be no confusion between the words and the action wanted. Having taught a dog to 'lie' on the command 'down', it is all too easy to say 'down' when you want it to stop jumping up, and besides producing confusion, it is unrealistic to think that a bouncing dog is going to 'lie down'. So you lost that round . . . don't lose too many! NO is useful for many acts of wrong-doing.

Come When Called
Coming when called should always be a pleasure to the dog from its very first days with you. While the pup is tiny, teach it to come to you when you clap your hands. Go down into a crouching position to greet the pup joyfully when it arrives with you to receive praise or a small reward. Coming when called must always be worthwhile to the dog, so that you never have

those embarrassing tussles with a dog which refuses to be caught.

When your dog is running off the lead, call it to you at intervals, not just when you are ready to put the lead on to go home. Call the dog for praise and petting and then let it run free again, so that the calling does not always end in a non-rewarding action of going on the lead. Some young dogs will tease by coming within a foot or so of your hand and then dodging away again. The remedy here is to attach a long length of rope to the collar; you can then step on the rope and reel the dog in, greatly to its surprise!

Playing retrieving games with a dog is best done with a home-made soft bundle of cloth, known as a dummy, rather than with balls or, worse still, sticks which can choke or injure the mouth. Always make the dog bring the dummy right to your hand. Never chase after the dog; it will always win, and while this may be fun once or twice it can develop into a 'dominating' habit on the dog's part, with you as the under-dog.

The action you are teaching must be properly completed before the dog is rewarded. If you praise when it is half-sitting, half-sitting is all you will ever get.

Formal teaching of this kind is best done for very short periods, several times a day, and not when the dog is anticipating some other treat, like a walk. Just before feeding is an appropriate time for a little drill, the puppy having to 'sit' and perhaps not approach the dish until you give the word. Your puppy's full attention will be on you at this time, so the lesson will sink in quickly.

It is a pity if you have to shut your companion dog out when visitors call, or if you cannot take it with you in the car, so try to accustom the dog to all sorts of situations as it grows up. Try to anticipate the problems that may occur and jolly the puppy along at all times. Do not forget the magic bean bag or empty drink can which helps you administer discipline from a distance. Do not, however, let the puppy play with this object afterwards . . . retrieve it yourself unobtrusively to use another time. You may have to have several bean bags at strategic points about the house.

Playing with dogs is fun and very good for adults too,

whose opportunity for foolish playing may be limited. Dogs enjoy hide and seek, hunt the slipper and other games which stretch their mental powers. You will find your dog enjoys solving puzzles . . . you may ask it to go through a door when the way is blocked by boxes, and see how the dog finds its own solution. The agility tests now often featured on television will give you ideas for ladder climbing, tunnel crawling and other agility feats.

Wrestling with big dogs can be fun for the young and fit, but it can be a dangerous pastime in that the dog can always win, and this is a very bad move for dominant or pushy dogs. In general it is better not to play rough games with big and dominant guard dogs, and never to let children do so at all. Never end the game in such a way that the dog feels it has won, always end the game when you say so . . . 'That's Enough' or 'Finish' can be the command, but say it calmly, not on a note of panic when you are losing the struggle. Reward the puppy when it stops on command. Tug-of-war games are very popular in big breed puppies, they play such games with their litter mates, but it is not a good move to put yourself in competition with the dog when the dog might win. Tugging and snatching can produce vicious tendencies in even quite young puppies.

Careful, thoughtful and consistent management of your dog will pay dividends later on. You should end with a dog which understands its position in the hierarchy and is a pleasure to own. Not only that, you get the reflected glory of knowing that your very agreeable dog, obedient but not cowed, is due to your own efforts. Let this be the best dog you ever owned.

Section IV

YOUR DOG IN ADOLESCENCE

15

GROWING UP

Puberty

Bitches and dogs reach puberty when they are between six and seven months old, although some bitches may be capable of breeding before that time or the large breeds may not be in season or on heat for the first time until they are almost two years old.

Males

In the male dog there is no obvious sign that this phase of their life has been reached, except that around this time the dog will perfect his leg-cocking action so that he can territory-mark efficiently. His early efforts will have been inaccurate and unsteady, to say the least.

At the beginning of puberty the dog may be seen to be trying to mate inanimate objects or even people. It is imperative to discourage this behaviour firmly and without delay otherwise it may build up into a major and constant problem in the adult dog. Immediate and effective deterrents are necessary at this time; the thrown object (beanbag or drink can with a few pebbles in) is particularly useful in these circumstances. During this stage it is unwise to leave the dog with children. In most dogs the hormonal levels causing this excessive behaviour adjust spontaneously over a few weeks or months and this behaviour will not be a problem again, provided you are not tempted into using the dog at stud even just once.

As we have said, the male should either be a career stud dog, with a steady supply of bitches coming to him or he should not be used at all. Since, unless your dog is a very big show winner, invitations to use him at stud will be very rare indeed, it is best to disregard this aspect of his life altogether. The very worst thing to do, when the dog is practising adolescent mating behaviour, would be to put him to a bitch at that time, although many owners think this is the solution to their problem.

You would also be most unwise to bring the dog into contact with an in-season, or about to be in-season bitch when this behaviour is occurring.

Young dogs that are just beginning to realise their masculinity may make more determined efforts to escape from your garden; re-double your vigilance, and check on the fencing. Keep the dog well exercised and occupied through this phase and that will make it pass more quickly. A large number of people have dogs which exhibit hypersexual behaviour because they were not properly dominated at this time, but there is no need for you to have one.

Fig. 13. How to reinforce dominance and enhance your status.
As pack leader, hold the dog as illustrated as part of the domination routine.

The dominance exercises illustrated can be used from time to time to show the dog he is not as important as he thinks he is. It is important to sort this problem out quite quickly as it can become very difficult to live with.

Bitches
The onset of puberty in the bitch is marked by her first heat or season, the period of time when the bitch is attractive to dogs and when she will allow mating. While bitches are said to come into season twice a year, the interval varies a great deal in individuals giving sometimes eight, ten, or twelve months between heats, although a bitch's pattern, once established, is usually much the same throughout life.

Fig. 14. How to show dominance.
Hold the dog as illustrated to show dominance.

Although bitches are usually rather excitable during their season, and just before it, there is not any marked change in temperament. Some bitches feel acute distress while undergoing a false pregnancy and they may be possessive or even aggressive in their efforts to guard a litter no-one else can see.

Understandable as this is, it is a very bad policy to sympathise with the bitch, because this reinforces the belief that she has puppies to care for. The best ploy is to jolly the bitch out of her broodiness, to give her more exercise and very little opportunity to retire to her bed with 'the puppies'. If she shows dominant behaviour, exert your dominance by putting her in a submissive position and holding her there. Stand over her and lift her front legs off the ground, make her go through her obedience responses several times and do not show her overmuch affection until she does something to your command. If the bitch becomes shy, retiring and nervous during her false pregnancy and nursing, build her up with plenty of praise and a lot of outdoor activity. Remove the objects she is guarding as substitute puppies discreetly. If you make a big scene about removing them you may lose!

While all this trauma may be avoided by controlling the bitch's heat by surgery or chemical methods, it is generally agreed that this should not be done before the first heat, but the first one is not usually so intense as those to come. Discuss the matter with your veterinary surgeon who will be glad to advise you.

There are a number of other inappropriate behaviours which may appear at this time as the dog reaches maturity. Males, in the large breeds particularly, may exert themselves and become defiant, probably as a bid for pack leadership. Your veterinary surgeon may advise medication, or possibly castration, if the dog's behaviour goes beyond what is endurable for your family. It is important to sort this problem out quite quickly as it can become very difficult to live with.

16

PREVENTION OF BAD HABITS

Excessive Barking

Barking is usually a protest against isolation or alarm barking at unidentified sounds or movements, but barking is also set off by the sound of distant dogs barking faintly. Barking and howling can be a response to distant members of the canine pack. If you leave a radio playing softly when you go out it may help to mask distant barking. Some breeds seem to find that continual barking comes easily to them, so the owner must not appear to go to the dog, even to reprimand it, as the attention of the owner may be rewarding to the dog.

Try to leave the dog alone as little as possible and for short periods only. To prevent excessive alarm barking, the owner should avoid stimulating the dog by excited commands such as 'Who's That?' etc. Alarm barking will almost certainly come naturally when the dog is mature and there is no need to stimulate this behaviour.

Barking at everyday non-threatening noises should be ignored, so that behaviour is extinguished, and the puppy can be positively taught by reward, to bark at exceptional events.

Nervous owners may find it useful to try to control their own 'alarm signals' when there is a knock on the door. If you 'jump out of your skin' it is understandable that the dog will pick up your fright reaction and make an unwarranted amount of noise. 'Stop', 'That's Enough' or 'Quiet' are useful words to teach to turn off barking which is prolonged, although most dogs manage to have the last word.

Barking while the owner is out can be a problem which grows out of a good thing. We want our dog to reveal its presence, to deter intruders, but we do not want it to go on so long as to annoy the neighbours. There is also the definite probability that a guarding breed, frustrated at not being able to do an effective job in turning the caller away, may destroy something in the room in order to work off its emotions. It may be that keeping the dog in a room where it can see the front door, and know the caller has gone away may lessen the frustration; it may also speed the caller's departure! You may have to use wired glass at the window as an angry guard dog will go through glass without a second thought. Another solution may be a notice (which can be bought at big dog shows or through the dog press), which gives a picture of the relevant breed and has the wording DO NOT KNOCK, I AM IN CHARGE HERE! This can be put into a front window when you are going to be out . . . it should not encourage burglars. The police say that a dog in the house is the biggest deterrent for the opportunist sneak thief, and the vast majority of burglaries are of this nature. The problem should not arise if you do not encourage overbarking in the first instance.

Stealing

As dogs do not have any moral sense, it is incorrect to speak of stealing in connection with a dog helping itself to food left around within reach. You can teach your dog not to touch its own meal until given permission, and you can also, by means of NO, stop the dog from approaching a box of sweets open on a coffee table, but remember the temptation is great if you are not in attendance. Magic deterrents work very well against opportunist 'thieves', or you may need to set up a situation so that you can use your planned deterrent.

Do not feed your puppy titbits from the table or, in fact, titbits at all unless it has performed some command. This is a counsel of perfection and if you have already established the habit of the dog begging and becoming ever more pushing while you are eating, *ignore* the dog, and insist that everyone else does so too. It may take a number of weeks, but if no human ever back-slides by giving the dog anything from the table, the behaviour will in the end be extinguished. On the other hand, how would any of us have got through our childhood without the dog at hand to dispose of those horrid bits of gristle which made so much trouble at meals? Where there are tiny children, prone to drop crumbs and crusts, it is very difficult to persuade the dog that it is not a good thing to sit close. You can order the dog into its bed in the same room until the meal is over, when it can have a reward for waiting patiently.

Excessive Biting

Excessive biting at the hands or ankles of humans usually responds to the standard methods of scolding or mild punishment at the time of the crime. These means should be tried in the first instance coupled by strong dominance procedures by the person concerned. If there is any sign that this treatment is aggravating rather than solving the problem, as it may just possibly do in a very dominant dog, the person being 'attacked' should stay quite still, not withdrawing hand or ankle. At the same time, or even before the 'attack', some stimulus that distracts the dog's attention should be applied.

Excessive Chewing

Puppies chew things as a way of exploring their environment and also to break down barriers between them and the place they want to be. The puppy chews as a natural behaviour, and when the second teeth are coming through, at about 4–6 months of age, the need to ease the mouth by chewing is quite evident. Puppies should be given one or two chewable objects, a log stripped of bark, a large marrow bone, or rawhide chews, and when a puppy is discovered at work on something else, the chew object should be substituted and the dog distracted on to its own object.

Dogs which chew doors when left alone may be cured by the 'remote magic method', if you come back when the dog thinks you have gone.

It is also possible to buy sprays (for example bitter apple) via the dog press which will prevent a dog from chewing a specific area.

It is a good practice never to make a big thing of saying goodbye to the dog when you are going out. Just see that everything important is put away and that there are some toys to chew and then go, whether for a long or short time. Emotional goodbyes only serve to prime the dog to know he is to be alone.

Submissive Urination
Until now we have principally discussed the need for the owner to become dominant over the pet, but in the case of the shy or nervous puppy excessive domination can lead to submissive urination, the kind of puppy that fills your shoes as you say hello to it. If you get the submissive urination response you will know that you have pushed punishment to its limit, or that you have a puppy that is right at the bottom of the domination chain so that it feels that it must make obeisance to everyone it encounters.

You must make immediate moves to restore or build up the dog's confidence. All corrective procedures involving deterrents of any kind should be stopped and the puppy should be praised and rewarded for all correct behaviour *and* for not showing inappropriate behaviour such as submissive urination.

Remember that a submissive dog of this kind should be 'jollied' rather than sympathised. Bend down to greet the puppy rather than patting it from above and let the dog take the initiative in greeting callers, but stop these tactics when you have reached a good level of confidence in the dog; do not let it go too far and into dominance.

Behaviour Induced By Other People
However well you and your family co-operate in managing the dog, you may find that bad behaviour patterns are being instilled and rewarded by people outside your control. It is not uncommon to find that neighbours are giving their scrap food to your dog through the fence. They will later on be very surprised and annoyed when the dog is barking there for attention and a free meal.

Similarly your dog may become over-excited and frustrated by children dragging sticks along the railings as they pass. You may be angry with the dog for damaging your flowers, but the impetus to do so was almost forced upon a dog protecting its territory. It is better to risk achieving a 'coldness' between neighbours by asking them not to attract or talk to your dog in any way unless you are with it, rather than have your good management ruined by people who do not have to bear the consequences.

It is not unknown for workmen, dustmen and so on to tease the dog unmercifully while it is young and then to complain of its aggressive tendencies later on. Supervision of the dog at all times is the best preventative.

Section V

YOUR DOG IN ADULTHOOD

17

CORRECTING INAPPROPRIATE BEHAVIOUR

Although the management of your puppy has proceeded well, there is always the natural tendency for the dog to develop new behaviour patterns which may be undesirable in your pack. You must be prepared to notice what is happening and to be ready to extinguish the behaviour before it becomes an ingrained habit. The following sections will also be of great help to those people who already have less than perfect pets, because the dog was obtained when adult or because the early training their dog received lacked purpose.

While studies made by animal behaviourists, particularly in America, have made it possible to establish a number of basic principles which can be used to correct inappropriate behaviour in dogs, it can be difficult to know the remedy to use in any one case. Every problem is different, the nature and physical capabilities of dog owners are different, the homes are different and the places and circumstances in which the inappropriate behaviours occur are different. Sometimes individual prescriptions for management are needed, and if, after following the basic advice given in this book, you feel that the problem behaviour is getting worse, or it is beyond you to dominate the dog, then we strongly advise you to seek professional help. Your veterinary surgeon may be able to help or put you in touch with a specialist in animal behaviour.

Because the results of an attack by a vicious, uncontrolled dog, even quite a small-sized dog, can be so disastrous, especially when children are involved, we strongly advise that you seek professional advice early where biting and attacking are the problem.

A behaviour problem that a dog has learned or acquired can be cured or at least reduced. The frequency of a behaviour will reduce if the behaviour no longer 'pays off' to the dog's benefit. If titbits are not given at the table the dog will eventually stop expecting them. But, conversely, the dog that has been trained to sit on command will lose that ability if it is ignored when it responds.

Dogs can feel rewarded when we do not intend them to, and many owners are unaware that they are reinforcing the very behaviour which they would like to stop.

The small dog which rushes to the front door, barking excitedly when the doorbell rings will have this behaviour reinforced if the owner strokes the dog, talks to it in what is believed to be a calming way, perhaps even picks it up into her arms before opening the door. All this is a rewarding procedure which will certainly register as 'paying off' to the dog, and it will be repeated at every opportunity. If this owner was aiming to teach the dog to bark wildly when the doorbell rang she could hardly do better! The dog will continue to lay on this hysterical scene in order to get its owner's attention. The appropriate corrective behaviour would be to shut the dog away and ignore it, or teach it some more acceptable form of greeting.

Another reinforcing behaviour often made inadvertently is an attempt to comfort a dog during thunderstorms. The dog is cuddled and fussed while it shivers and shakes, and the owner is conveying as strongly as possible to the dog that it is right to be afraid of storms because it gets its reward in special attention. In fact, excessive fear of thunderstorms is unnatural in the dog, and it is almost always generated by the owner who wants or needs a transference object for their own fear. It is noticeable that dogs which live in the flight paths of airports do not fear the noise of thunder, jet planes or fireworks, as noise is one of the everyday environmental happenings. This emphasises the need to acclimatise puppies to noise. Dogs are very easily conditioned to take up our own phobias. They watch their owners constantly and pick up our moods far more quickly than we realise. Especially where there is great devotion between dog and owner, a transference of fear is quickly made. If both dog and owner can jolly each other along, instead of sympathising, if they play a game, or put on some music, owner and dog can help each other out of a fear.

An even more bizarre conditioning happened in the case of an owner who had, since childhood, a great fear of small wild birds coming into the house. She was prepared to tolerate this failing in herself, but she noticed that her very large and stalwart guard dog was cowering under the table, shivering and casting horrified glances at a very cheerful little sparrow perched on the draining board. The owner realised that she had 'told' the dog, by her own behaviour, that the correct response to little birds was extreme fear, and the dog was showing this behaviour although a fear of birds is quite unnatural to dogs. Fortunately, the sight of so large and fierce a dog showing extreme submission to a sparrow served to point out to the owner how ridiculous and unfounded her own behaviour was. The need to bolster up the dog's confidence helped the owner correct what had been a longstanding phobia.

If your dog has acquired an inappropriate learned behaviour, think around the subject and see if you can identify how the behaviour or the measures you take to correct it have developed into a rewarding behaviour towards your dog. Consider that you may be generating the behaviour yourself. Remember: being comforted, given attention or even being grumbled at can be rewarding to the dog. Being ignored is never rewarding.

If your dog habitually does something which annoys you, consider using the counter-conditioning method. This means training the dog to acquire a new behaviour pattern, one which pays the dog better than the previous habit. For instance, if your dog barks hysterically when the door bell rings, you might try using a knocker instead, because high pitched sounds do excite dogs. You might also position the dog's indoor crate in the hall, and when someone is at the door, put him quickly into the crate, shut the door and drop in a biscuit. The dog may feel he has got a better bargain! Once a behaviour pattern has been disrupted, it is much easier to get the dog acting on different lines.

Remember, reward the dog very quickly for a correct response. Give verbal praise but back it up by a food reward. In the case of inappropriate barking, something to chew on can make all the difference.

The dog learns most quickly if the reward is forthcoming every time it responds correctly, but when the desired behaviour is established, give rewards only sometimes, so the dog keeps trying harder. If the behaviour is never rewarded, the dog runs the risk of losing the behaviour pattern you have taught him, but on the other hand, good behaviour does get to be a habit in the older dog.

A specialised technique can be used to break down anxiety or fear: exposing the dog to its particular fear on a very low level. The dog is rewarded when it can tolerate that level and then the stimulus is gradually increased until the full strength fear can be tolerated. It is similar to training people to tolerate heights: gradually being able to look down from a two storey building, then a five storey office block and right up to a tower block of many storeys.

A dog's fears are usually based upon lack of early conditioning to some factor, for example, car riding or the company of men, or an early bad experience, perhaps unavoidable pain at the vet's or a very strong punishment by a previous owner.

We rescued a dog which had a bold, even aggressive, temperament except for just one thing: she was terrified into a jelly by the sight or even the smell of a *feather*. We deduced that in her early life she had torn up a feather cushion and received drastic punishment. She was not, however, cured of destruction, but became afraid of cushions or even a stray feather on the ground.

We began counter-conditioning by putting just one feather within a yard of her food bowl. With reluctance, she would eventually walk in a wide circle all round the feather to reach her bowl, and she was praised for doing so. Gradually the feather was put nearer the bowl on successive days, and every time she endured its closeness, she was rewarded. If the fear persisted, the feather was not removed and the dog was ignored, but no other punishments or frighteners were allowed to spoil her day. She got no evident sympathy or petting which would have reinforced the fear. After quite a long time the counter-conditioning has worked to the extent that the bitch can sit on a feather cushion, but she will still avoid a stray feather lying in the grass. This behaviour is ignored.

Unreasonable fear of the veterinary surgery needs to be eliminated as a really frightened dog can set back its treatment and outlook for recovery. Desensitisation will need a positive approach and will make great demands on your time, but in this case, it will be well worth while. Begin by sitting in the waiting room with the dog for just a few minutes, at a time when there is no need to see the vet. Reward the dog when it can sit without fear, ignore it when it fails, and gradually increase the length of time you spend in the waiting room. Later on, the nurses and receptionists will be only too glad to take part by 'examining' the dog gently. Give each stage plenty of time and do not proceed to the next 'ordeal' until the previous one is tolerated with complete unconcern, and anticipation of the delicious reward. Lifting the dog on to the examination table is a big progression, but if you go when the main surgery is over, the vet will be quite happy to co-operate in breaking down the dog's fear.

The secret is to take desensitisation in very tiny steps, not going beyond what the dog can tolerate. Too big a step forward will ruin all the work you have put in, and you will have to begin at the beginning again. Everyone feels admiration for an owner who is taking a lot of trouble to cure a dog's behaviour problem in a constructive way, rather than following the too easy path of getting rid of the dog, so you should find everyone at the surgery only too willing to help you.

Correction
We have to let dogs know when they have done wrong, and sometimes with a dog of strong character, looking and sounding displeased is not enough. Corrective measures can be used effectively to stop undesirable behaviour if the following points are recognised:
1.   Correction can be done by means of 'shock' stimulus, preferably totally unexpected and out of range of the owner, such as the use of a thrown object or even a sudden, and rarely used, tap on the behind. Savage beatings degrade the person administering them and may make the dog even more determined to become dominant and even savage. Be

more clever than your dog! If you need to correct him, do it by using your brains, not your physical strength. Deprivation of your attention, ignoring the dog both in speech, action and glances may shame a sensitive dog, but another more happy go lucky character may not care a bit. It is up to you to know your dog well, and this will also mean that you know the deterrent which affects him the most. Having discovered this, do not use it too often, save it for really serious misdemeanours.

2. Correction must be administered immediately, which is why it is so difficult to correct some crime done while you are out. On your return it is too late to do more than look displeased, but the set-up situation of pretending to be out can provide the opportunity for more appropriate correction.

3. The corrective action must be strong enough to disrupt the inappropriate behaviour when on walks, or in the country, or when visitors are present, but the correction must never be so strong as to cause prolonged suffering and misery to the dog.

4. Correction is often not enough on its own. Ideally the dog should be taught another behaviour pattern which is acceptable, so giving the dog a chance to carry out another behaviour which will bring praise and a reward.

5. Shy and nervous dogs must always be 'built up' towards another behaviour pattern and never made more nervous by correction.

6. Puppies under 14 weeks old, at their most sensitive period, must not be corrected severely but always given the opportunity to do the right and pleasing thing.

7. Physical punishment that involves slapping an animal can be effective particularly when it comes as a surprise while the bad behaviour is being committed, but when a large adolescent dog is involved, it may be counter-productive as the dog may either fight back or take it as an invitation to play. Ignoring the dog and showing displeasure should always follow a physical slap. A sensitive dog, and most dogs are more sensitive than they look, can feel the change in atmosphere between its owner and itself.

If your dog commits a major disobedience while on a walk, for instance, you can put it on the lead, and 'turn off' immediately the pleasing sounds you make, put it in the car in silence, do not speak to the dog on the way home, etc. The dog well adjusted to its owner will notice the difference. Talking to the dog . . . saying, 'you were a bad dog, weren't you' *is rewarding with attention*, don't do it!

18

CURING SPECIFIC PROBLEMS

All behaviour problems in dogs need an individual approach but what you have read in this book will allow you to work out for yourself the appropriate way to look at any problem and to use the basic principles of behaviour therapy to select a remedy.

If the problem does not improve and you feel more help is needed, your veterinary surgeon will want to examine the dog to see if there is any clinical cause for the disturbing behaviour. It may be that the dog is hiding some illness or pain which is making compliance with your wishes very difficult.

Your veterinary surgeon can refer you to a behaviour therapist who is trained and used to sorting out behaviour problems in animals and it may be that in conjunction with medical treatment from the vet a solution can be achieved more easily than you thought possible.

Aggression

Because it would be so easy to make an aggressive dog even more fierce by the wrong correction it is advisable to ask your veterinary surgeon's advice before applying any remedial action.

A FEAR-BITER is a very dangerous dog indeed. This is the basically nervous dog which uses its teeth because it is unsure of its position in the pack and in the environment in which it lives. Unfortunately some rescued dogs turn out to be fear-biters because of incidents in their past life of which the rescuers and the new owners cannot be aware. Stern corrective measures must be avoided because this type of dog will turn upon anyone who attempts any physical correction. Your veterinary surgeon may suggest using a 'mood alteration' medication while your dog learns to trust his new pack.

Pain-induced Aggression
It is a natural reaction to pain to show aggression and any dog injured, for instance in a road accident, may bite the person who comes to help it. Some dogs which have had the experience of pain may become aggressive when they think they are about to be hurt. The best way to avoid such aggression is to take great care not to make the dog fearful. Some ear infections are extremely painful for some time even after veterinary treatment; it is only reasonable not to touch the dog at the head end at this time and to *warn everyone else*, especially children, that the dog is intensely sensitive in the ear region at this time. Grooming routines must be adjusted to tender areas and the dog should be liberally rewarded when it allows you to attend to a wound without protest. Punishment should never be used where pain is the basis for aggression.

It may be that you have not noticed a painful area on the dog so this is something which should be investigated when a normally even-tempered dog acts in an aggressive manner.

Learnt Aggression
Dogs can be taught to be aggressive but this is very seldom necessary in the traditional guarding breeds. Owners sometimes worry that the dog they bought as a guard seems to be everyone's best friend, but many of the guard breeds are slow to mature. They remain puppies up to two years old or even longer, and their guarding ability may never be overtly demonstrated, if the need does not occur, but unless you bought from very degenerate stock, the guard instinct will rise to the surface when needed. Some guard dogs need to feel affection for their owners and their home territory before they will guard; being ignored and not treated as part of the family pack can nullify the instinct to protect.

Guard instinct should not be encouraged and reinforced in large breed dogs which the owner will not be able to control should the aggressive tendencies become exaggerated; children should be especially warned not to encourage fierceness or aggression towards people or other dogs, even as a game. The situation could so easily get out of hand with disastrous consequences.

The more usual situation happens with the smaller breed dog, in the example visualised earlier, when the dog rushes towards the front door barking. Similarly, owners will often unwittingly train their pet to fight by being nervous that it may do so. On the approach of another dog, often quite a civil dog but one of a big breed, the owner begins to restrain and calm his dog, and may even pick the dog up . . . 'to prevent a fight'. They are, without knowing it, teaching their dog to be wary of other canines. Many dog fights would never occur if only the owners could have faith that the dogs will sort out their rank and role for themselves, if left to proceed without human interference.

Very dominant dogs should not be exercised in public places unless under strict control, and if they must be so exercised, they ideally should wear a muzzle, both as a warning to other owners and to prevent them biting. A dog will usually not pick a fight when muzzled. On the other hand, wearing a muzzle, even if only to protect other dogs, immediately gets *your dog* a bad reputation in the neighbourhood, and that is something you cannot afford to risk, since the Dangerous Dogs Act 1991 allows any person who feels threatened by or apprehensive of a dog to make a formal complaint to the police which may result in the dog being taken away and the owner prosecuted. As we know that 50% of the UK population do dislike or even fear dogs, it is obvious that we do not want to make our guard dogs look more formidable by putting them into muzzles.

Bicycle Chasing

Sometimes dogs become over-excited in a game and will attempt to chase children playing on bicycles. The dog is rewarded when the child pedals faster and the bicycle goes away. Children should be taught to dismount and to put the bicycle between themselves and any dog which is annoying them or showing aggression. The dog will soon get bored when the bicycle is no longer interesting. Another remedy is to arrange a 'set up' situation with an adult cyclist who will turn and direct a water-pistol stream directly at the dog. The dog, of course, should not be loose and thus able to harass cyclists so this behaviour is *the owner's fault!*

Car Chasing

Not infrequently, dogs wait by their home gate in the country and then set off at fast pace to chase a car that passes down the lane. The culprits here are often farm dogs of the Border Collie line, sublimating their natural and learned herding instinct by trying to round-up cars. Even if injury results the Collie is back at his ploy as soon as his limbs are mended.

This annoyance is the direct result of the old-fashioned notion, still prevalent in country and urban areas, that dogs can be allowed to be free and uncontrolled. In today's world, dogs must be fenced in or on the lead in public places unless they are in a completely safe area and fully under their owner's control while enjoying exercise.

Jealousy Between Dogs

Where there is more than one dog in a household, and especially where they are of the same sex and roughly the same age, it is not uncommon to find that aggressive feelings will lead to fights between the dogs. In this situation there is not usually any aggression towards the human members of the pack although in breaking up a fight, people do get bitten by mistake. However, even the fiercest fighter will desist when it feels its teeth go into human flesh, if that was not its target. The situation can often be cured by the owner enhancing his domination over both dogs by instigating regular training periods and making a point of holding the dogs in submissive postures.

In other situations, when the low toned growling starts which often heralds the beginning of inter-canine aggression, it may be more appropriate to stage a diversion, such as the owner walking away from the contestants ... or dropping an object causing maximum noise some distance away. Obviously it makes sense not to allow any 'property' to be owned by either dog, all beds etc. being communal. If one toy generates possessive feelings, it makes sense to remove it entirely, and to feed the dogs separately.

In some cases it may help if the owner reinforces the position of the most dominant dog, giving it privileges above the other, which should, in theory, be happy to have its submissive role defined for it. It may not sound fair to 'kick' the underdog and praise the dominant one, but in some cases the underdog is more contented and comfortable when it accepts its role in life. It may equally be true that the underdog will continue to make bids for dominance and the rivalry will simmer away for many years. Where one of these smouldering feuds exists, the dogs often take the opportunity to break into a fight when there is another excitement . . . visitors being welcomed is the classic one. If you know this is likely to happen, take the dominant dog with you to open the door, let it be greeted first, and then put away while the other comes out to be introduced. Two Boxer bitches fighting in the middle of the room are apt to wreck the best of cocktail parties! Surprisingly, the two participants in a long-standing war may be the best of friends for most of the time and the jealousy fights do not result in very grievous wounds, probably being more roaring than biting.

If a fight does break out, within the home or between unfamiliar dogs outside, it is important to know how to break it up with the least damage to people or dogs. Small dogs sometimes deliberately aggravate large ones, and the big dog's natural behaviour is to put the smaller down into submissive position. If only the owners can be persuaded not to scream, panic, or interfere, the smaller dog will eventually be allowed to get up and will walk away unscathed. It will be noticed that the 'victim' knows its own role quite well, and it will submit quietly; it is when people try to pull the aggressor away that the messages get all mixed up and injuries may be inflicted.

An evenly-matched fight is almost impossible to break up by physical means and people should be restrained from playing the hero and plunging in to try to open the jaws of one dog to make it free another. Subtle surprise acts best . . . a hose of water directed on the pair, even a car horn sounded loudly, the doorbell rung if in a house, all serve to distract the fighters, if only momentarily. The trick is to be ready to separate the two effectively at once otherwise your ruse will have been useless and the pair will be gripping each other again. If one dog is still on a lead, do resist the temptation to pull it up on its hind legs, revealing its soft under-belly to be bitten. Dogs normally take fight wounds on the neck and front legs and these are far less damaging than to the abdominal area or male sexual organs.

Fights in the kitchen, over a dropped crumb, can be broken up by banging a saucepan on the sink; any loud noise serves as a distraction so that one of the participants can be thrown outside. If the dogs are wearing collars, they can be induced to loosen their grip by the collar being twisted, momentarily, to choking point.

Jumping Up

Jumping up is probably the single most annoying behaviour which a dog can perform and yet, when it is done as an expression of pleasure and greeting it becomes very hard to curb. Essentially, jumping up is a dominant greeting, the exact opposite of the submissive action of rolling over and spontaneously urinating in your shoe. Jumping up may be cured by increasing the owner's dominant role, by stopping the reinforcement of the behaviour by allowing it to lead to a pleasurable experience for the dog, by diverting the dog's attention (counter-conditioning), by immediate reprimand and by very firm pushing down. It is important to make sure that pushing down does not escalate into a rewarding play situation in which the dog wins. All games that involve hyper-activity and rough play should be stopped, since they encourage jumping up.

It is pleasant to be greeted enthusiastically by your dog, but you will not want your best clothes ruined, nor will you want battering by eager paws when you are tired after work. Friends may not be so dog-orientated as you are and the action that you know to be an enthusiastic greeting may look to them very like an attack. If they react with fear, the dog is encouraged to take more aggressive action and what began as an expression of joy may end in an ugly situation. In summary the actions to take are:

1. First, teach your dog to sit and stay, using the learning principles as before, rewarding the dog with a morsel of food when it obeys . . . some people come home armed with a canteen biscuit just for this purpose.

2. Then be prepared to ignore any over-exuberant greeting, at the same time saying NO, or DON'T Jump Up (not down, which means another action).
3. Do not reward jumping up with praise, petting, pushing or kicking, which may be interpreted as a game.
4. As soon as the dog is calmer, tell it to sit and stay, reward obedience to this command promptly with food, not petting.
5. Once the dog has learnt to sit in such situations you can then walk towards it and, bending down slightly, stroke and pet the animal at the same time applying a downward pressure on the back over the shoulders.
6. An over-active dog may be distracted by giving it a glove or a purse to carry off to release its tensions . . . some people carry a special object with them for the purpose. It is not usually damaged, just carried about and may be tactfully retrieved later for use tomorrow.

Over-enthusiastic greeting is not a behaviour that can be extinguished easily or quickly, so it is better if you never let it occur. If from puppy days you greet your dog in a crouching position and put it through a domination routine if it shows signs of jumping up, you need not be put in the awkward position of having to train your dog out of being pleased to see you.

Destructive Behaviour

In some cases the natural instinct of the dog to investigate its surroundings with its mouth, which the dog uses much in the way we use our hands, is carried to extremes so that the dog will wreck the house or car when it is left in these places. As we have seen in the chapter on adolescent behaviours, destruction can be caused by frustration, and the need to work off emotional tension as well as when the dog is anxious, angry or bored, and sometimes from sheer mischievousness. Not all dogs are destroyers and it is not easy to see why some are and some not.

If your dog is already a destroyer, you will have to discipline yourself not to leave in the room with him any object that is easy to seize in the mouth and destroy. Everything portable must be tidied away before you leave and the rubbish bin must be emptied if you do not want it raided. Lonely dogs are particularly apt to pick up, and probably eventually destroy, any article recently handled by their owner so be forewarned to put everything of this kind out of reach.

It helps to keep the room where you leave the dog warm, and to have a radio playing, and you may want to leave a couple of toys which the dog has not used recently. It can also help considerably if you can arrange to fence off a small yard in the back garden and have a dog door constructed in the back door so the dog can get in and out of the house at will. This certainly helps with cleanliness in the house if the dog has to be left for any length of time and it also provides variety of situation for the dog. Don't leave any washing hanging on the clothes-line, this is a gift to the dog!

To be successful in circumventing destructive behaviour you must be prepared to progress slowly and to make sure the dog never succeeds in destroying things. It may take a lot of time and patience to work out this strategy, but it will almost certainly pay you to make a false departure and then come back very quickly to see what the dog is doing. But the snag is that the dog can smell your scent arriving. It is useful if you can get a clue to the trigger factor for destruction: does the dog start immediately you have gone, or only after a caller knocks at the front door or only when you have been away an hour or two?

There are dogs, and our new pet Sooty is one, who are extremely adept at opening the doors of kitchen cupboards. Some experts can even open up the refrigerator too. We are suspicious that Sooty must do a survey directly we leave, trying each door to see if it is securely fastened because if one is not properly locked, she will have that open and the contents out, even if it is a rarely used cupboard that is not on her usual list.

It may be worth while putting special catches on your cupboard doors and I know someone who ties a rope around the refrigerator. Best of all, rig up a booby trap, a pile of tins which will fall out directly the dog touches a door or a table top. The surprise element here is the deterrent; dogs usually jump away far too quickly to get hurt by a falling tin. Take special care to secure any cupboard which contains any potentially dangerous substances such as cleaners and disinfectant.

There are deterrent but safe sprays, obtainable from pet shops and through the canine press (bitter-apple is a well-known one), which put a nasty tasting but invisible film on woodwork which may stop gnawing of door frames and chair legs, but you may also want to upend the chairs on to the table top to keep them out of the dog's way.

Remember not to make a big thing of your goodbye when you are leaving, keep it brisk if you say anything at all. It is the 'hello' when you come back which can be joyous and prolonged with a food reward for the dog who has not done any visible damage. Dogs do get over the destructive stage, especially if they are not rewarded by finding anything interesting left about for them to destroy.

One final point: do not even consider putting the dog into the garden while you are out, because this is a real cruelty if the dog has no shelter from sun, wind or rain. In this situation the dog may bark excessively and it is as well to bear in mind that neighbours may complain and you, the owner, will be in trouble. You may think of installing a kennel in your garden for use during absences, so that the dog cannot do damage, but this, again, is not a good environment for a pet dog; you will not be teaching the dog anything, and you will lose the very useful intruder-deterrent of having a dog inside your house to protect your property.

Disobedience & Unruliness

There is a popular belief that dogs are not ready for training until they are six months old, probably generated by the many formal obedience training groups which have their eye on competitive work. It is a pity that this myth has become so strong, for many of the more energetic breeds are, by the time they are six months old, past the point of no return for early conditioning. It cannot be said too often that management, that is, training, of the puppy starts at the moment it becomes yours, and by the time the puppy is six months old it should be doing what you want it to do nearly all the time. A period of rebellion may set in during adolescence, but this is easier to cure when you have the basic foundations to build upon.

As with children, and in so many ways young dogs are like

young children, inconsistency of teaching also produces disobedience. The improper use of punishment, especially calling the dog in to be punished, produces a dog which will not come at all, for fear of what may happen to it. Corrective measures which the dog does not connect with the deed produce bewilderment, resentment, or plain non-co-operation in the dog.

It is quite easy to go to the other extreme and command the dog so much that it has no freedom of action at all. Some dogs will be submissive and afraid to move without direction, others may be rebels and delight in any opportunity to run off and defy their owner to catch up with them. The whole key to good dog management is to let life remain fun for the dog; let the good things happen and prevent, by your vigilance, the dog doing wrong.

Dogs and their owners train very hard, several nights each week sometimes, for the competitive obedience trials which culminate in top competition at shows. At these classes the dogs learn a set of formalised movements which are far removed from the things we want our dogs to do in normal life. If you wish to make obedience competition your hobby, by all means join a class with your dog, but keep up the management which you began as a puppy, it will in any case prove a good foundation for competitive work.

Lead Training
Large dogs which pull on the lead are tiring to take out and a nuisance to themselves and others. It is essential to train the dog to the lead *when you are not going anywhere* . . . on a separate occasion from an exercise trip. Choose a quiet stretch of road, and be ready to reverse direction every time the dog pulls ahead. The dog then finds itself behind you, and if you swing a rolled newspaper or stick in front of the nose the dog will be deterred from forging ahead. Keep the lead short, with the object of the dog being just at your side.

Your patience and staying power is what counts; reverse and reverse and reverse until the dog has got it right. Do fifty yards with the dog in the right position and then praise, reward and break off for the day. Repeat tomorrow and the next day until walking by your side is the dog's natural position. It can help to take a 'pulling' dog out with another one which has perfect manners in this respect. You may want to use the word 'Back' when the dog is pulling ahead, giving a significant jerk to show what you mean.

Pulling and bad behaviour on the lead can be cured.
1. Work at lead training when you have no objective in view except perfecting the dog's behaviour.
2. Do not try to train when the dog is going for its walk.
3. Persevere, and reward!

Car Sickness
Car sickness can be genuine motion sickness, in which case it will be necessary to seek a veterinary surgeon's advice and suitable medication. Beware of using preparations intended for humans, even in children's dose: the canine reaction to these medicines can be quite unpredictable and frightening. If you are carrying your dog in the back of an estate car, you may find it a salutary experience (if you are prepared to take the extra risk in the event of an accident) to try a short ride as a passenger in the dog's position. There can be a great deal of vibration in the luggage space, enough to cause discomfort to the dog. Some dogs ride more comfortably on the floor of the car where they cannot see out.

It may be that car sickness is the expression of a phobia arising from a bad experience. Tigger very much enjoyed car rides until he had the misfortune to be thrown from a car which was in a minor crash. Tigger ran off across country and by the time the drivers had sorted themselves out he was nowhere to be seen. This dog, a very well adjusted companion animal, obedient and properly dominated by his owner, for the first time in his life refused to come when called. Although he did not travel far from the crash site, he took shelter in woodland nearby and deliberately avoided all attempts to recapture him. After twelve hours of fruitless calling and searching, Tigger's owner sat down in a neighbouring field and just waited quietly, knowing that he was in full view of the dog which was hovering in the shelter of trees. Eventually, after a long wait, Tigger very tentatively made his way to his owner, who wisely made no move to catch the dog but spoke gently and encouragingly all the while.

This anecdote is told to show how quickly a long-term trust can be shattered by a traumatic incident. We cannot know how the car crash affected the dog; it may have seemed that his owner 'threw' him from the car as a punishment. It so happened that Tigger had guilt feelings at the time of the crash, as he normally travelled in the back seat, but had ventured into the front, knowing it was against the rules. His owner had decided to ignore the behaviour 'just this once' as they were nearly at their journey's end.

Although it is wrong to assume too much human-type thought in a dog, it seems quite likely that Tigger felt the car crash was a punishment directed at him, and in that case it was decidedly an over-punishment. The story also points to a moral of never allowing a dog to do what you know to be unsafe or wrong, even for a few minutes.

Tigger was unhurt after the crash and not exactly frightened, but better described as disorientated, as if his whole world had crashed about him. If in fact he had regarded the crash as a punishment, this might well have been so.

To continue with his story, he was soon riding again in a hired car quite happily, and we congratulated ourselves that he had not developed a car phobia. This happy idea was shattered when the crashed car was returned to us; Tigger absolutely refused to get into it, and although he was dominated and made to ride in it, and in a successive model of exactly the same type, he never enjoyed car riding and had to be made to accompany us every time. Eventually, we got a car of different make and shape; Tigger got in willingly and is now a very keen motoring dog again, so if your dog has a car phobia, it may be with good reason, and a change of car could help.

The carsick puppy should be taken out for short rides as often as possible, logically before meals instead of just after. If the puppy drools or vomits, no comment should be made; certainly no sympathy given. In the end puppies, like children, outgrow car sickness if it is virtually ignored, but giving attention, even by turning round constantly to see how the dog is faring, is an encouragement to the dog to vomit, as this species does easily. Make the car ride short but enjoyable by going to a place where the dog can have a walk, not only a trip to the vet or the poodle parlour or to wait in the car while you are shopping.

If you acquire an adult dog which has never had experience of cars, allow it to sit in the car while it is stationary, then to be in the car while it is backed in and out of the garage and so gradually lengthen the drive, but be *jolly* about it, not anxious and sympathetic to the dog. If you have your dog in the garage with you, take care that there are no pools of antifreeze about; this substance is sweet-tasting and very attractive to dogs, but it is a deadly poison.

When the dog first goes out in the car, have someone hold the dog steady if it is a lightweight. Being jolted about is unpleasant for humans *and* dogs. Yorkshire Terriers as a breed tend to be poor travellers and they are best carried in a crate, obtainable in wood or plastic and very useful in many ways for tiny dogs.

If the dog persists in car sickness and there is a long journey to be undertaken, seek advice from your veterinary surgeon about suitable medication.

Shyness
A shy dog is often one that lacked proper socialisation during the sensitive stage of puppyhood, probably through not meeting a sufficient range of people. A dog may also become shy as a result of too hard punishment not correctly administered in relation to the dog's behaviour. Punishment which the dog cannot understand can provoke a fear reaction which may take the form of aggression, or extreme submission, expressed by involuntary urination and evacuation.

If this should happen you have direct evidence that your management (or that of a previous owner) is wrong and too harsh for the particular dog you have. All punishment should be stopped and the dog's confidence built up by everyone in its world. The dog should be played with frequently and the dog should be shown the value of interaction with people . . . being friendly should 'pay off'.

Some dogs are almost permanently 'shy' with visitors but are composed and happy with members of the family pack. If it is desired to extend the dog's range of accepted humans, the newcomers should avoid talking to or even looking at the dog.

Eventually, after hours, days or even weeks the dog's natural curiosity will allow it to approach, and a food reward should be forthcoming instantly. Visitors should be asked not to call or otherwise to try to attract the shy dog, let it come of its own accord. It can help if a newcomer takes the dog for an enjoyable walk, making this a socialisation period but not, of course, letting the dog off the lead.

The Boisterous Dog

The dog that is too boisterous, too anxious to welcome visitors can be a great source of annoyance and even embarrassment. The temptation is to shut the dog away but that does not solve the problem, for punishment by isolation may make the dog hostile to callers or it may lead to room destruction through frustration. It is not easy to put the dog through a domination routine when people are entering the house and claiming your attention, and it is not easy to get visitors to behave as one would wish, neither fearing the dog nor exciting it.

One of the best solutions is to shut the dog away until the visitors are welcomed and *seated*, and then to allow the dog to come in, asking visitors not to call it or even concentrate their attention on the dog. The dog will want to investigate the callers and there seems no way around this; any lively dog will want to get the scent of visitors to its pack. The dog should be controlled by the owner so that its approach is as calm as possible, and after a few minutes the dog can be commanded to go to its bed and it should be re-ordered back to its bed if it makes itself a nuisance. Visitors must be asked not to fend the dog off (that is, initiate a play routine), or to give it lumps of sugar or biscuits 'to go away'. We know that the reverse action will result.

One word of warning about leaving mature guard dogs with visitors to the house (e.g. babysitters). Although extremely pleasant when the owner is at hand, these dogs may drop into a different role when left in a room alone with a visitor. The dog, apparently so relaxed and sleeping, may emit low warning growls if the visitor moves about the room, picks up magazines and books etc. . . . the dog is putting its guarding into effect as well as it knows how. The dog should not be reprimanded . . . in fact, the owner may not know that this behaviour takes place unless the visitor complains, and few do . . . but care should be taken to remove the dog while the owner is away from the room, unless it is suspected that the visitor needs watching.

Guard dogs can also be resentful of visitors walking about the house or garden, although friendly to them while they are sitting in one place. Owner domination and care that the dog does not have the opportunity to harass visitors will save this from becoming a problem. Especial care should be taken of child visitors whose shrill voices and running movements may be outside the experience of a guard dog normally accustomed only to adults.

Licking

Excessive licking of human hands is a sign of submission, often demonstrated by a dog which has been reprimanded for dominating behaviour as a signal for re-admission into good status within the family pack. 'Don't Lick' is a command which can be used, while removing hand or face from licking range. Puppies lick their dam's mouth as a signal for her to regurgitate partly digested food for them, and also as a submission sign to dominant dogs. This face licking may be continued in their first home, to children especially. This behaviour should not be allowed and the puppy should be distracted by some other stimulus.

Shaking Hands

This is a submissive action, but one that is attractive and endearing, and it may well serve as a safety valve to the boisterous dog when visitors call. Teach the action, with suitable verbal cue, after the puppy has learnt to sit on command. You can teach older dogs new tricks too!

Inappropriate Eating Habits
Coprophagy

Some dogs begin in puppyhood to eat their own or their litter mates' solid excreta. If as tiny puppies their enclosure is not cleaned frequently, this behaviour may start, prompted from motives of investigation, play or possessiveness. In some species, notably rabbits and newborn foals, it is normal to eat the faeces of others, in order to acquire bacteria to aid the digestive process. The dog appears to find nothing repugnant about the performance, and perhaps this is a survival habit going back to pre-domestication. Not all dogs eat their own faeces, but it is not uncommon in young dogs. As the cause is not known, the cure will turn on trial and error, but always:

1. Remove all faeces from the garden as soon as passed.
2. Keep close observation on the dog at all times. A dog with this problem should sleep in the owner's room, as if left in the kitchen there may be hardly any evidence that faeces have been passed and reconsumed. If the dog wakes you to go out in the night, at least you can prevent coprophagy becoming an established habit.

If caught in the act the dog should be firmly reprimanded (NO, or thrown object). Otherwise, the behaviour should be ignored and other remedies for the condition should be sought.

Suggestions which may be tried, one at a time:
1. Extra bran or vegetable fibre in the diet.
2. Your veterinary surgeon may be able to suggest a remedial diet or possibly medication.

Eating The Faeces Of Other Animals
Dogs are attracted to eat the faeces of cats, cows, deer, rabbits, horses and other animals. They will also pay far too close attention to fields on which slurry has been spread as fertiliser.

This eating habit is entirely undesirable, as there is the possibility of transmission of disease, or worm eggs; the dog will almost certainly vomit at some time afterwards, and its breath will smell. It is very difficult on a country walk to prevent the dog discovering a pile of fresh horse manure while it is off the lead. NO said loudly as you see the dog's head go down, the thrown object if you are near enough, and calling the dog to you and praise-rewarding may be the answer, but most dogs will snatch a mouthful or two before they come running to you.

Prevention is the best method, dogs should always be led across fields that have recently been inhabited by cows, and take care that their heads are held high by a short lead. The contents of cat litter trays should be disposed of efficiently so that the dog cannot exhume them.

Eating Houseplants
Dogs will eat houseplants, sometimes from sheer mischief, or else as a substitute for the grass which they would eat to some degree in the wild. Some houseplant leaves are poisonous, the Christmas Poinsettia being one of the most dangerous so these popular plants must never be left within a dog's reach. If this urgent need for a grass-like substance occurs frequently, seek veterinary advice.

Eating Vomit
Dogs vomit easily, and some will bolt their food and bring it back undigested, only to eat it again with pleasure. We may feel revolted, but the dog seems to enjoy this action, which should be ignored unless the eating and vomiting cycle is frequent, when veterinary advice should be sought.

Window Dressing
Dogs which rampage at the window when other dogs are passing are territory guarding, sometimes much more fiercely than they would dare to do if they were able to confront the invader. It is an activity which breaks up the dog's inevitable boredom, and it is a matter for the owner to decide whether this 'pleasure' to the dog should be allowed. If it is, clear the window sill to allow the dog easy access, as it is often those articles which are knocked down which eventually get destroyed. Some dogs which are destructive through boredom have been cured by constructing some kind of window seat where they can sit and watch passers-by thereby adding a great deal of interest to their day.

Hypersexuality In The Male Dog
We must recognise that to keep dogs singly within the boundaries of our own gardens, without sufficient exercise (few companion dogs get as much exercise as they are capable of taking), without the company of a canine pack and interaction with bitches is to keep them in an unnatural state. Domestication imposed a massive adaptation on the wild dog and modern conditions of living have imposed even more. We would not have it otherwise, for to let a dog run freely now is not only

unkind but anti-social and against the law.

The male dog has had to modify its sexually orientated behaviour almost more than any other species and we have to realise that instinctive aggression towards other males, mounting behaviour, and territory marking, have become the only expressions of sexuality left to the companion dog. Compulsive wandering, excitability and destructions are secondary mood expressions which may also be due to hyper- (excessive) sexuality in the companion dog but all these signs were only normal in its free-living ancestors.

Behaviour Demonstrations Of Hypersexuality
1.   Aggression.
2.   Mounting other dogs, people, or inanimate objects.
3.   Territory marking, especially urination about the house.
4.   Roaming.
5.   Destruction.
6.   Excitability including excessive barking.

A recent survey taken among the owners of male dogs showed that well over half of their pets were performing some of the hypersexual behaviour patterns mentioned, very often at under twelve months old. This means that in the general dog population at least half are not a pleasure to own and they must be a source of embarrassment if not an actual liability to their owners. Few of the owners, in fact, complained of their dog's behaviour, taking these sexual expressions as part of the package deal of owning a male dog, and this may be the reason why bitches are by far the most popular choice of pet today, especially now that medication or spaying is available to control their seasons.

There can be little doubt that most of the traits which we term hypersexual are normal in male animals and it is merely a question of place, severity and frequency which makes this behaviour unacceptable. It is not really known what causes some males to be more sexually active than others but theoretically it could be the excessive production of male hormones or malfunction of those parts of the brain, the cerebral cortex, which controls sexual function. In many cases the undesirable behaviours are wholly or partly learnt and result from incorrect management by the owner. Poorly or inconsistently applied corrective measures in early life could be to blame and often such activities are promoted by unwitting reinforcement by the owner.

Behaviour Modification To Correct Hypersexuality Traits
Make sure you are not 'encouraging' the dog by mild punishment, which may be construed as a reward. Mounting is a dominant behaviour so increase your leadership role and lower the dog's position in the hierarchy. If the dog is mounting specific objects, remove them. Petting and fondling should be avoided and food rewards substituted. Avoid exciting the dog by games but give sufficient walks. When the dog shows the slightest signs of beginning a sexual behaviour, distract it by throwing a toy, for instance, and then go on to give it a dominating training session. It is best to avoid all punishment in this regime as it will generally be ineffective and may lead to aggression, though the thrown object is useful where territory marking is excessive.

If the hypersexuality is a learned response, the co-operation of all the family in the above regime should extinguish the behaviour. If the dog continues to be a problem in this way, see your veterinary surgeon. Medication or castration may help in some cases.

Section VI

CHARACTERISTIC BEHAVIOUR

19

OLD AGE

The life expectancy of dogs varies tremendously, being influenced by shape and breed, and by long-lived strains within that breed as the tendency to live beyond the average age is hereditary. Bulldogs are among the shortest lived of our dogs (seven to eight years), followed by the very large breeds (Danes and Mastiffs), and then by Boxers and Dobermans where a life span of ten to twelve years is a good average. In general, the smaller breeds tend to live longer and Spaniels, small Terriers and crossbreeds are among the longest lived dogs, fourteen to fifteen years being reached by many individuals and some going on until nearly twenty. It follows that Bulldogs are going into old age when Cockers are just in their prime and Boxers, which remain puppies a long time, are just settling into reliable maturity. With advancing years dogs, like people, begin to suffer with problems associated with chronic diseases and degenerating body function but after many years of happiness with your dog you will not grudge the extra care and consideration it needs in old age.

Sight
The dog's sight degenerates with old age but also from a number of eye diseases to which the dog is prone, such as cataract. Blind or semi-blind dogs manage very well indeed on familiar territory, indeed you may not realise how little your ageing dog can see. When you realise its sight is failing, do not move the furniture around or leave hazards like wheelbarrows across the garden path. When you notice that your dog cannot see a ball or

is bumping into things, get veterinary advice quickly. Ophthalmology is just one of the many areas of veterinary science which has made great strides forward in recent years.

A dog which tended in its youth to be aggressive with others may become more so when handicapped by failing sight, particularly when one eye is out of use and it can be taken by surprise from one side. You may have to keep such a dog on a lead in public parks.

Hearing

Some dogs become deaf with age but this matters relatively little as by the time your companion is deaf it will need few commands because it will be adjusted to doing what you want as a matter of habit. You may have to devise a system of hand signals, waving a white handkerchief will do, to attract the dog's attention from a distance. You will, of course, have a special care for blind and deaf dogs on roads and cliff top walks and in other hazardous situations, and you will take care not to let the dog be startled out of sleep.

Incontinence

Incontinence, or rather what the medical profession calls *frequency* becomes a problem in the ageing dog, which may find it impossible to go through a ten-hour night without passing urine. It is usually only in very old age, when the dog is failing that it will pass urine in its sleep, soiling its bed. You may find that you have to set up a routine similar to that of puppy days, either taking the dog into your room so that it can wake you when it needs to go out, or you can cover a small area of its sleeping quarters with newspaper which it can use. It is extremely unkind to withhold water during the evening in the hope of keeping the dog dry at night and to do so can be damaging to the kidneys. Before you accept that night frequency is due to ageing, do ask veterinary advice, since dogs suffer with cystitis and kidney problems, which may clear up quite quickly after treatment and your dog will then be back to 'lasting all night' again. As the older dog will by now be immediately responsive to your wishes, it is little trouble to let it out to be clean frequently, saying your special code word. Some old dogs do not suffer from frequency, but when they do have to pass urine it has to be done as quickly as in puppy days; be ready to adjust to your old friend's needs and never, never blame because it cannot behave as it did in its prime.

Teeth

Some breeds lose their teeth quite early in life, Cavaliers and Yorkshire Terriers being among the earliest, at about six or seven years sometimes, but they can still manage quite hard biscuits. Very aged dogs may appreciate their food being put through a liquidiser to make a smooth consistency; tinned dog food is excellent this way.

An old dog can be given almost a new lease of life by the removal of decayed teeth and some attention to the gums and oral hygiene by a veterinary surgeon. Removal of pain, sometimes shown by drooping of the ear on the affected side, gives an added interest in eating and the dog becomes altogether more lively and, incidentally, much nicer to be near. It is a great pity to have to reject the advances of an old friend because of halitosis (bad breath), when a vet can do so much to cure the condition.

Indigestion

Reduced muscle tone in the intestine together with less inclination for exercise makes old dogs more prone to digestive troubles, and also to flatulence and 'noises off' which may prove embarrassing in company. The larger breeds are especially inclined to producing tummy rumbles and obnoxious odours, and even worse, they have this awful way of walking away from the smell giving their owner reproachful glances as if to accuse *them* of defiling the atmosphere. There is little remedy but to laugh it off! It may pay to make a change in the diet; even a change in the brand of tinned meat can make a difference.

Arthritis

Arthritis is commonly seen in old dogs, but there is so much help which the vet can give them that the arthritic old dog is rather better off than a human sufferer from this condition. Dogs can take the pain relieving drugs which sometimes have to be denied to people because of long-term side effects. You may notice that the old dog grunts with pain as it gets up, and limps or staggers for the first few steps; that is the time to seek veterinary advice. If your dog has been covered by insurance for veterinary fees since its youth, the cover goes on until the end of its life, so that your dog can have all the benefits veterinary science has to offer to make it more comfortable. An ageing circulatory system makes the dog feel the cold more and it cannot move fast enough to keep warm. A short-coated dog may need a jacket to put on for its last trip into the garden at night in cold weather; get one that covers the chest as well as the back. Make the old dog's bed especially soft; you will notice that heavy breeds get callouses on elbows and hocks which can become very sore if the dog lies on a hard surface. Polystyrene-filled bean bags make excellent beds for arthritic dogs, providing warmth and support for aching joints. The arthritic dog must not be hurried; have patience while it gets out of its bed slowly to answer to your call. Take care not to bang into the dog not too steady on its feet when it first gets up and, above all, get veterinary advice to keep it pain free. Your friend may have several happy years with you yet.

Heart Disease
Heart disease in dogs is usually shown by a chronic cough and an inability to take much exercise. Be suspicious of the dog which is no longer keen to run and sits down while it is out. Your veterinary surgeon can prescribe medication to support the heart's action which will help your dog.

Obesity
Middle-aged and old dogs tend to become fat. Excessive weight brings with it many problems: breathing difficulties, liver disease, intolerance of hot weather and skin troubles. Do not wait until your dog is old and overweight to think of slimming it down, it may then be too late because the body's metabolic rate slows down and the dog does not burn off so many calories by exercise. Prevention is better than cure; watch your dog's food intake in relation to its activity throughout life.

Many veterinary surgeries run obesity clinics with regular weighing and advice.

Management

If your management of your dog through puppy days, adolescence and adulthood has been good, perceptive and consistent there should be no need to talk of punishment in the dog's old age. Your dog will be living as you want it to and good behaviour will have become a habit. Old age is the time for indulgences and pampering, even perhaps letting the dog dominate you just a little. The matriarchal Boxer, Pooka, at eleven years old is demanding, autocratic, has us jumping at her every bark, thrives on privileges the other dogs do not get and we would not have her any other way. The cleverness of old dogs is something to be enjoyed, it is a very special attribute of their later years.

20

CHANGES IN BEHAVIOUR PATTERNS

Because you are so familiar with the behaviour patterns of your dog you will have the advantage of knowing when those patterns change from the normal *for your dog* and so you may be able to recognise the onset of a disease before overt signs show. It is as well to bear in mind that dogs will behave differently when they are feeling unwell or have pain, so seek veterinary advice early. You will then spare your dog a lot of suffering and misunderstanding and will have a much greater chance of getting the condition cleared up quickly.

Aggression

Sudden aggression in a normally placid dog may have its origin in *pain*, possibly an abscess forming, impacted anal glands, chronic ear conditions or toothache. Brain disorders associated with epilepsy, infectious disease and tumours may cause dogs to become unnaturally aggressive. It is always wise to seek veterinary attention if a normally pleasant pet shows sudden bouts of bad temper. Try to work out any associated factors which may help the vet in his diagnosis.

Hyperactivity

Dogs with a mild degree of over-activity of the thyroid gland (hyperthyroidism) may become nervous and irritable as well as over-active and the problem may become extended to extreme restlessness. If you have a too active dog, be sure that its behaviour is not being encouraged and reinforced, especially by children. If you cannot identify the cause of the behaviour, consult your vet. Possibly an adjustment in diet to provide less protein may help.

Self Mutilation

Some dogs suck at their paws and pull lumps out of their coats, even destroying themselves down to the flesh and causing wounds which are very difficult to heal. The cause may have been originally one of irritation or a foreign body, but like children picking at spots, the dog goes on working at the site as a means of relieving tension or boredom. Veterinary help will be needed to institute some regime of medication to induce the dog to leave the area alone so that healing can begin or the original cause can be corrected. You may also be shown how to bandage a different part of the dog's body so that its attention is diverted.

Coma

Diabetes, liver disease, inflammation of the kidneys and abnormal levels of essential minerals in the blood can lead to coma, or to hyper-excitability. Such dramatic changes in behaviour require professional help so that the exact cause can be established and the appropriate treatment given.

The Bitch

Bitch owners should be prepared for the changes which affect temperament to a greater or lesser degree during the hormonal cycle (the season and subsequent false pregnancy and nursing). Each bitch varies in the way this time affects her: she may become more excitable and demanding, or more lethargic, may refuse to eat, or may be short-tempered and disinclined to co-operate with her owners, but the changes are usually minimal and should be accepted as far as possible.

If the behaviour is very much exaggerated and the bitch tends to become very difficult at this time then there is a good case for controlling the heat either by having the bitch spayed or by medical means. These changes are not learned, so they do not lend themselves to behaviour modification techniques.

Aggressive protection of puppies can be aggravated if a bitch feels threatened by other animals or unfamiliar humans approaching her puppies too closely. As with every other attribute, bitches vary in the strength of their maternal possessiveness; some will allow other bitches, usually their mothers or sisters living in the same household, to lie with them and help take care of their puppies. Others will guard so intensely and be so busy warding off real or imaginary threats that they will fail to nurse their puppies adequately. It makes sense for the owner to arrange that the newly whelped bitch is kept in seclusion from human and animal visitors for the first two to two-and-a-half weeks after the birth. In kennels it is not unknown for one bitch to invade the nest of another and kill all the puppies. The aggressor very often has a similar aged litter of her own, so nursing bitches must not be kept within earshot of another litter, as the noise of other puppies seems to excite bitches unreasonably.

Some bitches are very particular about which of the human pack may attend to their puppies, and they may make aggressive moves towards a visiting veterinary surgeon at this time. Although owners would like a photographic record of the litter, the presence of a photographer often excites and upsets the bitch. All handling of nursing bitches should be as tactful as possible to avoid upsetting the bitch at this sensitive time, and it should not be assumed that, because a bitch is normally friendly with some human or dog, she will allow them to approach her when she has puppies.

Conversely, some bitches lack maternal instinct to greater or lesser degree; some are easily distracted away from their puppies and the extreme condition is unwillingness to pay the puppies any attention and not even to be willing to stay in a bed with them. The latter condition may have some painful cause, either the bitch has a condition of the uterus which is making her feel ill, or perhaps the nipples are too sore to allow the puppies to feed. The remedy may be as simple as cutting the puppies' nails; scratching the teat area can be very painful to the bitch. Because good mothering behaviour is essential to the survival of the offspring it is important that breeders do not use bitches with either of the extremes of maternal behaviour described, however closely such bitches may, in external appearance, approach the ideal for the breed.

21

CONCLUSION

In the space of this small book it has not been possible to cover all the inappropriate behaviours that may occur in dogs but we hope that we have succeeded in giving enough help to owners and prospective owners of dogs so that they may apply our principles to their own particular difficulties. If you are in doubt or find that the techniques which we advise do not work, even when you apply them with diligence and co-operation of everyone in contact with the dog, then seek professional advice without delay. Do not be afraid to turn to your vet for help, he should be your friend and counsellor on all matters appertaining to your pets.

Veterinary surgeons are obliged to provide 24 hour cover to look after animal emergencies. It is usual for neighbouring veterinary practices to combine this service in the evenings and at weekends. Telephone any veterinary surgery to receive a message about which one is open for after-hours work.

Do not expect that a veterinary surgeon will come out to a dog injured in a road accident. Now that so much sophisticated equipment is available to help injured or sick animals, it makes more sense for the dog to be carefully transported to the surgery where the vet and a nurse can start treatment immediately, but always telephone first to make sure where to go.

Alternative Medicine
Homoeopathy is increasingly used with success to treat dogs, and more vets are studying this alternative therapy. Your own vet may suggest these treatments or refer you to a veterinary surgeon who has gained extra qualifications in this art.

Laser therapy and acupuncture are also available for suitable cases.

Specialist Vets

There are now extra qualifications in many branches of veterinary medicine which are acquired after considerable study on the part of veterinary surgeons who are interested in a particular aspect of injury or disease in animals. When a case needs deeper investigation than the local surgery can provide your vet may refer you to 'a specialist' or you may ask for such a referral if you think your pet will benefit. These consultations and subsequent treatments are covered by most comprehensive pet insurance policies.

Our ultimate aim is to help you to make each puppy and dog you acquire into a successful companion which will be in your home for the whole of its life. If, by writing this book, we can do something to alleviate the enormous numbers of pet animals which are discarded and eventually destroyed every year, we shall feel it was all worthwhile.

If you follow the management techniques described with patience, perseverance and perception, you will have a dog which is a pleasure to own, a dog that will be admired and envied by all your friends.

Jim Evans, owner, with his wife, of Anna, the Doberman, knows that you will say with truth 'My Dog is Better than Your Dog!'. Kay White, owner of Pooka, Berry, and many other Boxers, and Harold White, owner of Tigger, know you will get as much pleasure and fun as we have had from all the dogs which have lived with us.

APPENDIX

Useful Information

The Kennel Club   1 Clarges Street
Piccadilly
London W1Y 8AB
Tel: 0171 495 6162

Dog registration, list of Puppies for Sale, information on Dog Shows and also the address for *Kennel Gazette*, a useful and informative magazine published monthly.

Weekly newspapers dealing exclusively with the canine scene:
Dog World and *Our Dogs* – available from newsagents.

Colour magazines providing addresses from which to acquire solutions to every canine need, including wire crates (indoor kennels), beds, coats, etc.:
Dogs Today, Your Dog and *Dogs Monthly* – from newsagents.

List of puppies ready for sale: Pet Plan Puppyline
Tel: 0181 580 8183

Insurance proposal leaflets are displayed at your veterinary surgery.
Discuss the alternative proposals with the receptionist or the veterinary nurse.

INDEX